The
Responsible
Suburban Church

Books by GAYLORD B. NOYCE
Published by The Westminster Press

The Responsible Suburban Church

The Church Is Not Expendable

The
Responsible
Suburban Church

by GAYLORD B. NOYCE

The Westminster Press
Philadelphia

ISBN 0–664–24902–7

LIBRARY OF CONGRESS CATALOG CARD NO. 71–110724

BOOK DESIGN BY
DOROTHY ALDEN SMITH

Published by The Westminster Press ®
Philadelphia, Pennsylvania

PRINTED IN THE UNITED STATES OF AMERICA

128234

To my parents,
Harriet and Ralph Noyce,
whose love for people
and for the church
has so helpfully shaped
my own pastoral instincts

Contents

Contents

Preface

Back in the '50s a white Southern minister addressed a regional gathering of white Southern laymen and spoke passionately on the race issue. He thought he was risking his own career, let alone all rapport with his audience, but he was determined to speak his conscience. As he ended his address, a man rose from the back, choked with emotion. "Pastor, we know you're right," he said. "What we want to know is, what shall we do?"

Moving rhetoric about the crisis in the cities and about the suburban church has its place, but in these strident times rhetoric has not been wanting. The time comes for sober, unexaggerated assessment of the realities and for that second step that helps along the man who wants to know, "What shall we do?" Enmeshed in large-scale institutional structures and social patterns, serious-minded and moral men want help with just such a question on a scale that they can handle without giving in either to a sense of futility or of panic.

It is my hope in these pages to do more than offer some interpretations of the persons and social issues that confront the suburban congregation. I would hope to offer practical guidance while avoiding the faults of a cookbook approach to the tough job of Christian witness and mission in suburbia.

That I had time to complete this manuscript is the result of a faculty leave given me by Yale University in 1968–1969, and for this I must express my deep gratitude. Equally, I am indebted to the Dean and the faculty of Harvard Divinity School, where I studied and wrote during that year. In reflecting upon suburban churches the following ministers, unnamed in the text or notes, have been of help to me: Allen Holt, Imre Kovacs, Harland G. Lewis, Donald J. MacCallum, R. Winthrop Nelson, Jr., Roger Nicholson, Richard Rangoon, David J. Robb, William T. Scott, Jr., and George Todd. One layman I should mention is Horace Besecker of the Boston City Missionary Society.

I have exploited the patience of my wife, Dorothy, for help in smoothing out my more awkward attempts at translating ideas into readable prose; she deserves a reader's thanks. Finally, two generous secretaries, Mrs. Susan Williams and Miss Jane Wheeler, have provided efficient assistance.

G. B. N.

New Haven, Connecticut

I | The Church and Our Move to Suburbia

1. A Revolution in Community Life

The urban crisis of the late '60s created a profound problem for the American suburbanite and for his church. The suburbanite felt out of it but uneasy, guilty but unsure of what he should be doing. Government aid, church action, and academic research were for the time concentrated on the city itself. Now, however, serious reflection about the suburbs is in order.

America is going to the suburbs. The central cities are not growing; many are actually losing population. The countryside holds its own at best; most counties of the country decline in population decade by decade. Population growth is concentrated in suburbia, and suburban growth means political power. Elevated incomes represent economic power, and highly trained personnel from the suburbs make major decisions about the life of the cities.

It would be naïve to think it easy to redirect this suburban power so that it better serves the welfare of the central cities. The Social Gospel often assumed that it could convert top-level power to righteousness and thence could reform the social order. When church leaders in 1919 waited upon Judge Gary of U.S. Steel and proposed to this Christian layman an end to the 72-hour week in steel, however, they were simply heard and then dismissed.[1] It took a massive exposé of the system, a mobilized public opinion, and the agony of more labor strife to shorten the work week. The Social Gospel, knowing the worldly implications in its Christian faith, matured only when Reinhold Niebuhr added to it realistic insights about self-deception among the righteous and about the place of political power alongside persuasion as a means to social change. In the years ahead cities will often lock horns with suburbs in political and social struggle.

It would be just as naïve, however, to neglect the potential resources for change within suburbia. The power of the suburbs today is very real and it must be taken into account by strategists and practitioners of church mission. Knowing *how* to fix up the inner cities is of little use if the suburban majority holds back the financial means through its control of Congress or church councils and community funds, or, worse yet, if they turn in backlash upon protesters in the city and take more repressive steps.

A working definition of suburbia partly deflates the suburban myth of high incomes and easy living in an oppressive mass society. The myth has been attacked by Bennett Berger, Robert Wood, Herbert Gans, William Dobriner, and others. Berger studied a working-class suburb to prove, for example, that suburbanites are not all the white-collar and junior executive types that the myth had pictured, and that the Park Forest of *The Organization Man* is not the only style of life for the suburban family. Wood reported that in 80 out of 106 suburbs studied blue-collar breadwinners ranged from 40 to 100 percent of the gainfully employed. Gans lived in Levittown, New Jersey, for two years beginning from its inception and found suburbanites to be typical Americans whose life in suburbia was a continuation of their life before the move. It was not a move into the upper middle class. Nor was it a move into "fresh air slums" as represented in one of the novels that helped build the myth—*The Crack in the Picture Window*—where developments are characterized as "conceived in error, nurtured by greed, corroding everything they touch until they drive mad myriads of housewives shut up in them."

Our definition of suburbia need not be statistically precise, for this is not a sociological essay. This book deals with the work of the suburban church and its participants. We use suburbia in this book as a symbol of a cultural change that is more significant than political boundaries on a map. If suburbia connotes a style of life or a set of attitudes, this book may be inapplicable to some congregations set geographically in "suburbia" as defined by statistics from the census. Some "suburban" churches have many of the characteristics of city or even inner-city congregations. On the other hand, many a middle-class congregation, while technically a part of the city, may find it profitable to move through the kind of thinking represented in these pages.

A review of what the church is up against and up to in suburbia has something to say about the church's business in the whole culture. Suburban style is a component in the cultural image of the good life. It influences churchmen who live elsewhere.

We could easily argue that all we have anymore are cities, core and periphery, all parts of a single reality. (For that matter, we can study larger units, the coming "regional cities" with their exotic names: Bos-Wash, San-San, and the like.) To a certain extent, we make that point in this book. Were that the whole story, however, the word "suburbia," its mythology pared off, would connote nothing. Yet suburbia represents a definite element in our society, and it is possible for us to study this particular segment of the church's life and mission.

Our boundaries for defining suburbia will be four.

1. A suburban community is one that is primarily residential and is cut off by political boundaries from the central city. Moreover, suburbia is at a distance from the places of work for the preponderant number of its residents.

2. Suburbia is primarily middle class, as contrasted to "inner city," low-income areas. ("Middle class" is, of course, a highly ambiguous term. Many of those the sociologist would call the upper middle class think of blue-collar residents as "working class." Most blue-collar workers, however, regard themselves as middle class and share many of the same aspirations, in terms of their living standards and mores, with the "higher" group.) Suburbia is a community from which the extremes of poverty and great wealth are generally absent.

3. The suburb is a community with a certain psychological distance from the city proper, a sense of being "out here" instead of "in there." A few minutes listening to conversations about the social problems of the metropolis or about the place of work will reveal the strength of this suburban trait. Community associations, separate from city organizations, reinforce local suburban identity.

4. The suburb is dependent upon the central city in significant ways beyond commuters' paychecks. In meeting its needs for cultural resources and leisure-time activities, for air and rail terminals, for higher education, for major commercial functions, the suburban community is not self-contained. It is a satellite community.

Two exceptions to 1 and 2 must be noted. First, increasingly, suburban communities attract light industry into their lairs; industry follows people out of town. The number of persons working within the suburban community is increasing; a man often drives to another suburb when he goes to work, rather than into the central city. This is a long-range trend. From 1930 to 1950 suburban New York increased by 50 percent in population. The number of commuters to the city went up by only 20 percent. Suburbia is less and less a simple dormitory place.

Second, some suburban communities have within them a genuinely low-income population at the fringe of community life, a fact that may surprise the congregation which takes the trouble to look at its community census data, and which may provoke some modification of the image the community holds of itself. Michael Harrington's characterizations of the "invisible poor" can apply to those elderly persons, migrants, workers, or old-timers who happen to live on "out back" but within the political boundaries of some suburban communities. Older "suburban" towns with populations of over 30,000 share many of the social problems of the central city while the town's self-image often denies it. The result is a shortage of social services and of strategy to attack the social ills.

Three changes are represented by the move to suburbia.

Numbers. During the '50s, the metropolitan areas of this country accounted for the overwhelming preponderance (88 percent) of American population growth. However, in these metropolitan areas, the areas outside the central cities grew much more rapidly than the city proper. These suburban areas increased their population by a remarkable 46 percent! Over a third of the cities actually grew smaller. The real growth was in suburbia. Altogether there are fewer people today within the 1950 boundaries of the central cities than in 1950! More of the people in these metropolitan districts now live outside the city than within it.

William Dobriner calls this move to the suburbs the second major revolution in American community life—the first being the move (late in the nineteenth century) from the country to the city. In terms of sheer numbers this was probably the largest migration of people in so short a time in all history.

Another resurgence of the housing boom is anticipated for the early '70s as the post-World War II babies enter the job market, marry, and raise families of their own. The cities being filled, these new families will constitute a second wave of the suburban explosion.

Style. America is going to suburbia in style. Suburbia is home for what David Bazelon calls the "new class" in America. If in days past the crowded central city was the living place for the workers of our industrial enterprise, the spread-out suburban area is preponderantly the living place for the technicians, managers, and marketers of our new technological era. The machinist and the electrician live in suburbia in increasing numbers, in the smaller homes, but another class is outnumbering them. In this respect suburbia reflects a shift in the American work force. In the thirteen years before 1964 while employment grew by ten million and our industrial production rose by half, we did not even expand our *blue-collar* work force. This remarkable trend continues. In terms of income, the American work force no longer represents so much a pyramid as a diamond, with a smaller lower fifth in poverty, tragic enough for those involved, beneath the bulging middle-income groups.

The mind-set of white-collar suburbanites is highly significant for the direction our nation moves culturally and politically. David Bazelon calls these people "the decisive swing group to mediate and perhaps finally to resolve the classic American conflict of the city-dweller and the small-town agrarian, the immigrant and the WASP." [2]

When we look seriously at the values and the responsibilities of suburban residents in later chapters, such possibilities for these "new men of power," to borrow a phrase originally used of an upper managerial group, will be our further concern. The most typical successful man is not now the landowner—the original elitist before the industrial revolution. Nor is he the holder of corporate wealth—the "capitalist" of the nineteenth century who brought money and technique together. Nor is he the banker or the labor leader who manage yet other sections of our economic resources, "factors of production" in classical economic terms. He is one of the group technocracy whose members contribute their skills to the large team that is the basic corporate structure in the new industrial society. He is adman, market analyst, product designer, and vice president for this or that in the production hierarchy. Or he is a professional —doctor, lawyer, professor. Alongside these men are only a few who manage their own small businesses in the retail and service lines. The ramifications of this shift for the American ethos and its implications for the church's ministry highlight the urgency of our concern for the suburban church. These pacesetters live in suburbia.

Social responsibility. Even more significantly, America is in danger of moving to the suburbs in a figurative sense, off to the edges of moral seriousness. This is a cultural accusation highly difficult to assess. No generation is easily compared to another, least of all in its sense of moral responsibility. What is at issue warrants our concern, however, if it is only a significant possibility.

America's "second revolution in community life" has split our population geographically into "two cultures," as

William L. C. Wheaton puts it. Like a giant centrifugal milk separator, we have spun off three quarters of our population from the central cities, those who have been able to cope successfully with the demands of contemporary living, and we have left behind in the inner city a quarter who have not been able or have not been allowed to do so well. "Out of sight, out of mind" has come too close to being the result.

A modern nation's evolution to true greatness is to be measured less by the achievements of the many than by its concern for those who don't "make it." That our medical technology and affluence in this country yet leave us, for example, only eighteenth among the nations in terms of life expectancy, is a reflection of the poverty we still allow in our society. The move to the suburbs has left concentrated in the central city the economically, medically, and socially handicapped.

This nation has been a leader in public education, but the system at present, gives too little evidence of such concern in the inner city. Our concern for education has "moved to the suburbs."

We are enlightened enough to call our penitentiaries "correctional institutions," but we are still told of cruel neglect and bestial vengeance inflicted by our society upon those unable to live within the law or unable to buy the legal defense that earns light sentences. We seem more concerned to throw the book at the lawbreaker than to rehabilitate the offender. Our concern has "moved to the suburbs."

A nation that has doubled its real per capita income in the generation since World War II, and that after that war poured out Marshall Plan and Point IV aid to the rest of the world, now steadily snares the underdeveloped nations

with loans instead of grants from its expanded wealth—
even that at a very limited level. Development aid for the
world's "southern" half is high on the agenda of almost any
knowledgeable observer of the international scene, but
such aid goes lower and lower on the list of American priorities. The "two culture" phenomena on a world scale in-
tensifies; relatively the rich get richer and the poor get
poorer. We see being laid the groundwork for Mao Tse-
tung's revolution of the rural areas of the world against the
rich "city" nations. If suburbia in any sense symbolizes
complacency, America gives evidence of moving to suburbia, turning in upon itself in foreign policy.

Correlating such a tentative observation of our national
mood, as we move into the '70s with the trend toward suburban living, is risky prophesying at best. The validity of
this line of argument will come clearer only as we touch on
the value structures nourished by suburban culture. Nonetheless, such breadth of concern augments the need of the
suburban soul for the responsible suburban church.

The suburbanite is neither an immoral escapist, running
from responsibilities in the city, nor the ideally happy
American. He has been accused of the first by much of the
literature on suburbanites and he has been idolized as the
latter by slick magazines.

What has the suburbanite done?

1. He has sought housing that he could afford, for one
thing, and often it has turned out to be located in a developer's tract. Ticky-tacky though it may seem to the out-
sider, it is home for the new suburbanite. It is his own.
Federal subsidies of various sorts have helped account for a
massive increase in suburban home ownership, and it is
ironic that many of the beneficiaries of this assistance now

resist similar aid to a new and less fortunate generation of urban dwellers.

The rise in home ownership represents one of the most significant changes in our society. In the early '30s, only a third of the families in this country owned their homes; by the mid-'50s, two thirds did.

2. The suburbanite has also sought the best that he could find for his family. The best seemed to be the suburb. Again, this is a commendable assumption of family responsibility, much as it is also a correlate of the privatism that has prevented broader social concerns among many suburbanites. Christian ethics does not legislate a particular family structure. Gallup's announcement that 62 percent of American husbands help with the dishes *can* be called emasculation of the male; it can also be called an asset in terms of the family structure and a reflection of a Christian and cultural concern that attributes to the woman more personhood than did a former generation.

3. The suburbanite has sought community rootage. Often he has been transplanted—by higher education, by war, by hunting work when the opportunities were limited in his hometown. Rootage in a place may be called baalism (Harvey Cox) and "town culture"; certainly nostalgia for a bygone style of life plays some part in the suburban exodus. The demonic potential in the search for community must be acknowledged; the word *community* is warped when it becomes an excuse for closing off entry to one segment or another of the population and when suburbia turns into a defensive enclave. Search for human community, however, is response to a basic human need, and if suburbia provides it in some measure, we can be grateful.

Suburbia is made up of people who, for the most part, are similar to the rest of the population—people seeking security and fulfillment in the ways that seem open to them, going about it often aggressively or selfishly or defensively. What these facts say to the church charged with lifting up the life of man into the light of God is our next concern.

2. THE ONE THING NEEDFUL

As does any other, the suburban congregation needs to know something about the general mission of the church before it can judge what difference its particular setting makes for its strategy.

The empirical church throughout history has engaged in amazingly diverse activity. It has fought wars against the infidel and the saloonkeeper. It has run schools and nursing homes. To this day it is training ladies how to care for toddlers and for fur coats. It entertains men's clubs with films of last year's football season, and teen-agers with the latest rock records. It preaches about Jesus. It attempts to engage the culture in social reform. It holds hands and pours tea and sells potholders at church bazaars. What then is essential in the church?

Worship as a paradigm. In the midst of all this activity, the most distinctive identifying mark of the church, past, present, and—although this is more debated—future, is the activity of worship. We can of course attempt to explain church attendance in other than religious terms. "People really go to church for reasons of sociability or prestige," "to show off their Easter clothes," "to meet their friends." Nonetheless there is a distinctive quality to meaningful worship, mixed as it may be with other motivation. This activity of religious man is basically different from our gathering in political conventions, baseball parks, and the rituals of fraternal orders. This is true in spite of the fact that both laymen ("My lodge is my church") and scholars ("Political and religious gatherings alike integrate individual and society") know that the distinction is not absolute.

Worship is an end in itself. Therefore we treat worship inadequately if we interpret it only as simply hearing a message or as a pep rally where we stir up enthusiasm for social service, the "real" work of the church.

Worship is a paradigm or model for what the church is or should be up to in its other activities. This does not mean that piety will always be expressed in the present forms. It does mean that the unifying concern of the church through all its manifold activities is the active assertion of the God-relation which is the context for human life. In worship we assert and celebrate the Christian understanding of life in various ways—by singing hymns, by giving voice to prayers of confession and intercession, by reading and expounding "God's Word" in a rehearsal of the "revelation" through which God addresses man. We do the same in the Sacraments, and in offering symbolic gifts (sometimes all too symbolic) of loyalty and support for church mission.

This assertion is also made in other important ways, however. We point to the God-relation in activities of evangelism that bring people and the tradition of faith in touch with one another, whether the language is "Christ died for your sins," "Blessed are the peacemakers," "Capital punishment and Christianity are incompatible," or "I want you to visit our church." More strikingly, wherever the systems of society tear life apart, dehumanize it, or leave its potential unrealized, we express the God-relation by social action that reflects the Christian conviction that human life is knit together under God.

People of the church do more than "assert the God-relation" as you would assert a mathematical axiom. On the one hand, in both worship and social action, they enact the God-relation in an *expressive* way as the poet puts to verse his feelings, strengthening the while the unity of their own lives in this truth. On the other hand, with *intentional* strategy, churchmen endeavor to share that truth with the world and move the world toward the Kingdom of God.

Church as event. With some justification, Jesus is remembered as one who came with a verbal message: "The Kingdom of God is at hand," "Repent and believe the gospel," "Judge not that you be not judged." Jesus was a preacher and a teacher. As one reads the Gospel accounts, however, it becomes clear that Jesus' words were inseparable from a style of action, one that offended the "best" people and gave meaning to what he said. Jesus' parables were often spoken to interpret and defend actions such as his association with the disreputable outcasts of his society, the poor, the tax collectors, the women of the streets.[3] The conclusions of such stories as that of the Pharisee and the publican in the Temple, the prodigal son and elder brother, or the laborers hired late in the day were a stinging rebuke to the righteous and self-righteous, the "best people" of his own time. These people were not unlike a moralistic suburbanite who is so preoccupied with "law and order" that he has little concern for economic justice and rehabilitation of lawbreakers.

Jesus came not only with parables but with parabolic action. Likewise the church is in the world not so much as a loudspeaker or a textbook but as an event. It is called to be a community such that its participants sense the God-relation and such that it is an occasion for change in the world around it. The world is to be healed as well as addressed. Thus the church acts in the world with parables (preaching, study groups, teaching, publishing) *and* with parabolic action (liturgy, deeds of mercy, action for social reform) .

I define the church in this way to clarify something that puzzles many people in a day when the church is increasingly activist. The church is continually being urged to join its institutional power to movements for civil rights, mental health, urban renewal, peacemaking. All these activities are inevitably of concern to the church and they become major aspects of its parabolic action. But *ad hoc* voluntary groups and political organizations are at work on them all, so people ask, "What sets the church apart?" In pressing that question they express a correct hunch that the church has a distinctive vocation.

In the church we express one major truth—that our lives and the world's life are lived out in the context of God's creative and redeeming will for the world. The skeptic finds no context for human life but the decaying objects and transient events that meet the eye. He sees the individual projected into life against a blank canvas. The Christian, however, begins with a sense that life is given meaning within a God-relation; it is not a meaningless existence in a void. Elaboration follows after such a statement, of course —what or who "God" designates, whether He is "out there" or "in here," living or dead, the significance of Jesus Christ in giving content to the assertion, and much, much more. All of that is subject to discussion and modification within the Christian community. What the bare statement rules out, however, is total skepticism as to the seriousness of human life and final despair as to its meaningfulness.

Church as intentional community. As we live within this frame of reference, human life becomes intentional, purposive. It is no random tale "told by an idiot . . . signifying nothing." The God-relation elicits from us a response of action and decision, so frequent a point of the parables.

The Christian is called not only to rejoice in God, to "enjoy him forever," but to responsibility, "to glorify God" with his life. The "good news of God" reclaims life from "aimlessness" as one contemporary creedal statement puts it. It places life on moral ground. It makes it human, for subhuman life is amoral, lacking that intentionality.

This intentional pattern in human life is important for comfortable suburbanites to understand. If life is defined materialistically, the suburbanite has it made. He has food enough and shelter and a high degree of physical security. He does not have it made, however, in terms of something to live *for,* not until he is moved by larger purposes. Jesus told the rich young ruler, a prosperous, law-abiding "suburbanite," to sell what he had and give. The church is called to help persons express and mature in Christian intentionality.

Putting the matter in this way, however, can lead to despair unless the full richness in the Christian understanding of the God-relation is comprehended in the life of faith. If intentional striving to love God by serving man represents an essential part of human fulfillment, what is to be said when we recognize the extent of our failure as persons and churches to intend the good? Are we not condemned to despair the very moment we suggest that the Christian life is identified by its intentionality? There is always more we could and should intend. Do we not end up with a counsel of frenetic activism rather than one of joy and hopeful love?

For these reasons we must make it clear that the one thing needful in the Christian church is not in the first instance a revolutionary program of social reform, even if that be seen as a logical imperative deriving from the God-relation. We must begin instead with reflection upon the paradox of judgment and grace and apply it to the suburban congregation.

The paradox of grace and judgment. The assertion that man exists in the God-relation is both a word of grace and a word of judgment. In fact, it is a word of grace in part by virtue of being a word of judgment. It looks with suburban man, for example, at all those objects in terms of which he often hears the good life described, and it judges them. It suggests that they are not the whole story—the new cars, the happiness images associated with a brand of cigarettes or deodorant, the self-help procedures of popular psychologism, or the gregarious good times at the barbecue pit. The assertion suggests that there is deeper reality to be known either in spite of all this or mediated through it. As the cross reminds us, the gospel acknowledges the twistedness of our life, hidden even behind the bland or pleasant suburban contenance. It knows how easily a man can be seduced into thinking that in the backyard swimming pool and the half-acre lot his larger hopes will be fulfilled. The gospel is a word of grace because of this acknowledgment.

Thus, the encouragement of the gospel is much more than a "chin up" pat on the back. Jesus does not say to the weeping prostitute in Simon's house (Luke 7:36-50), "Don't carry on so, you're really a very good person at heart." He says, "Your sins [they are many, he admits] are forgiven." The church, set among all the smiling faces of suburbia, is engaged in very serious business. By judging aimlessness and sin, it comes with a healing word that offers to shallow happiness or aching desperation, something of joy and peace.

For such reasons, the news that we live in the presence of God can be a terrifying word to us. It brings condemnation of the empty ways in which we may be squandering our life; it brings judgment on our subtle exploitation of one another or of the world around us.

We often resist with an almost unbelievable tenacity the truth about ourselves because of the threat it represents. If crutches have held us up—an inflated esteem for our own abilities or a denigrating view of our neighbors—we resist losing them. The possibility of finding ourselves wrong in our estimate of reality—whether that estimate has to do with the free enterprise system or Black Power or our own ambitious importance—is a personal threat. Yet questioning the crutches is one way the church mediates to the culture the good news of God. Judgment leads to change and healing.

Because of our resistance to the wholesome truth that judges us, it is even more important that the church assert the other half of the paradox, God's grace. No man can afford to learn the truth about himself (he will find a way to resist) unless he can trust someone's love for him as he ventures into this unknown process of dropping the crutches. This is true in marriage relationships, in psychotherapy, and in owning up to the sorrier facts about our own lives. Grace is essential if we are to have courage to confess our weakness; we can dare to know ourselves only as we realize we are loved. "Your sins are many," said Jesus to the woman, *"but they are forgiven."* Indeed, Jesus went on to imply that she, being forgiven, could love others as Simon, unaware of his need for forgiveness, could not.

Crutches and revolutionaries. Suburbia presents us a lifestyle in which crutches are easily come by. Because of the crutches it is not difficult for others to imagine *sham* written all over the day-by-day life of middle-class suburbia. Such revulsion characterizes sensitive bohemians of any age, and our own is no exception. However, outright rejection of middle-class life-styles is often rooted in a highly romanticized version of what life can really be, and it is important to recognize this illusion for what it is. The failures of utopian experiments, just as the disappointments of lovers who overidealize marriage, only confirm Christian insights summed up in the hoary doctrine of original sin. Men live richly in community only by virtue of repeated repentance and reconciliation, not by some perfect arrangements of social structure or of marriage vows.

Nonetheless, it is important to recognize the kind of sensitivity that prompts youthful and bohemian rebellion. Many patterns in suburbia do not fulfill human life. The large measure of our actual sham and the extent of our misguided, narrow-minded good intentions partly account for the negative connotations many now find in words like middle class, Establishment, suburbanite, housewife, businessman.

The church must take a hard look at the suburban lifestyle, noting the poses and the crutches, if it is to do its job of asserting the depths of life that they obscure. In its social criticism, the church is not prompted by romanticism or neurotic alienation, but by a balanced love both for the suburbanite himself and for those in the world beyond suburbia, many of whom are hurt or unhelped as a result of the crutches or greed in suburbia. Healthy love for people acknowledges their poses, their normal need for crutches, their fallibility and sin. Healthy love also knows that the grace of God can work for change and wholeness. The church acknowledges both the good in good intentions and the evil in them: the mother's child-rearing concerns, partly warped by "smother love"; the deacon's loyalty to the church, partly an escape from a nagging wife; the "irreplaceable" executive's 80-hour commitment to the firm whose success he believes to be important to his employees, a commitment that he blindly allows to destroy his wife and children. Even these faulty intentions may express for individuals their sense of a moral claim on life. Even these intentions may mediate and express something of the God-relation on which to build a faith more free and full.

Similar ambiguities characterize the institutions that comprise the social order and frame our human life—hospitals and business corporations, courts of law and trade unions, factories and universities, voluntary associations and family units. These collectives appear often to be so self-seeking as to defy facile statements that they live "under God" and serve human need. Yet human life is sustained by social organization and the church is called to act not only in relation to individuals but also on the social level, seeking to interpret and influence the life of such institutions in the light of their true vocation.

The posture of the congregation. The suburban congregation has a moral responsibility to the life of the entire metropolis. It does not follow, however, that we are called on to launch at the suburban congregation a set of ballistic missiles—injunctions as to what it *must* do—or that the church should use this tactic in its ministry to suburbia.

The Christian faith represents the God-relation as gospel—good news. God is for man; man is delivered from estrangement, despair, and guilt, into a living relation with him. The gospel comes as health to a sick man, as food to the starving, as guidance to the lost. The prior response of the Christian, therefore, and of the Christian congregation, is gratitude and joy. The root motivation for service and obedience is responsible thanksgiving, quite different from a fearful doing of duty for the sake of self-justification. Our injunctions to the suburban congregation are to be offered in this spirit: "Seeing that we have this gift, shall we not do this or that, in celebration, and as response to God? Seeing that we are bound by ties of loyalty and gratitude to him whose will is this justice and that mercy, shall our humble walk with him not be in this or that obedient way?"

We do not specify the content of mission for any particular church. For many a small congregation "parabolic actions" may be little more than offering a loving concern to those lonely and isolated individuals who fall between the cracks in a broken world, people cut off from normal ties to family and neighborhood and fellow workers. Such deeds by the church embody and express good news.

For the stronger suburban congregation, however, the mission usually involves ties to the city, if the congregation and its suburban community are to learn what their true situation is and begin to assume a responsible relationship to the real world roundabout. This is the opportunity for that congregation which begins to find its life turned in upon itself, with no good news to offer. An individual can be emotionally sick even if well fed and physically secure if he has not moved with his moral self into reciprocal and purposeful relations of love for others. It can be the same with the suburban congregation that thinks there are no problems "out here"—no poverty, no race problem. The health of the suburban congregation may be renewed in its discovery of mission. The motivation for the mission, however, is to grow from joy as much as from a sense of duty.

"I don't believe I can come to church anymore," said a parishioner just back from a long and renewing experience of work abroad. "People are always pushing me to do this or that. I would prefer simply to worship." Assured that the church was born in freedom from "pushing" and the law, this woman attended worship after all. A year later she herself was initiating through the church a children's summer recreation program in the arts.

To put the matter in quite another way, without any thankful ecstasy religion's good works are hollow. In one poster, Sister Mary Corita splashed out in her bright colors words from e. e. cummings: "damn everything but the circus." Joy in God's love undergirds our mission.

What are the people of a congregation to do? Not anything, *necessarily,* save to come together in the name of Jesus and see where that leads them. There will be seasons when attendance goes down, and the nights are cold, and all that seems to happen is that the Sacraments are received and the Word studied and rehearsed. That is enough. This is the one thing needful. A church is the poorer if many numbers do many things under its roof but if nothing of the activity expresses the God-relation which is most concisely articulated in the preached and enacted Word. During its leanness, a congregation may live in trust, if the Word is there, that new life, phoenix-like, will again arise for the health of man—man of city and countryside and suburb alike. That life may well express itself in a new sense of mission, and to several aspects of suburban church mission we now must turn.

II | The People of Suburbia

Introduction

A number of perspectives shed light on the distinctive tasks confronting suburban congregations. We will use three. In this chapter we examine certain problems faced by persons in the suburban context. In Chapter III we look at several social issues relevant to the suburb and to its church. In Chapter IV we consider some mission strategies for suburban churches. None of these pretends to be exhaustive. Each illustrates the kinds of concern that a suburban congregation may develop as it evaluates its own ministry in the light of its situation.

One warning is necessary. The church's ministry in the world involves concern for both the individual and the culture. The two are inseparable. No man exists in a vacuum; from society he derives his speech, the images through which he perceives the world, and the motivations that guide his actions, even while he remains a unique individual. As an individual he helps constitute the society from which other men, in turn, derive their lives. The danger of selecting one kind of *social* setting for analysis is that the personal ministry of the church will be neglected. In this book we assume the personal ministry in every congregation—the pastoral counseling, the mutual concern and care of member for member, the quiet witness of faith to faith, the normative and central activity of worship. Most ministers and parishioners answer on this personal level if they are asked about the most meaningful part of their day-by-day service in the church. For example, one suburban pastor wrote as follows:

> What is meaningful to me and I think to most of the core group of the laity with whom I serve here is the possibility in the church of more than superficial personal relationships; more than the casual careless associations one has in the world. The church offers a more intimate, supportive caring fellowship than one can find most places in society.

This ongoing personal ministry is a vital part of the life of any congregation, however, and is not an exceptional function of the suburban setting. Therefore it will not be a focus of attention in this book. I do not mean to play down these personal dimensions of the Christian mission in setting forth perspectives related to the particular social setting in which suburban congregations find themselves.

In the following three sections we begin with people. All kinds of people live in suburbia, but certain ones are more typical. Among them are those on which we base these sections on youth, on women like Mary Browning, and on "men at work." We might instead have spoken about children, about the elderly, about families as such, but these samples will serve to help us think about the people of suburbia.

1. YOUTH

There is little need to stress the existence of a youth subculture within our society. Both the popular press and the trade journals rehearse the millions of dollars of spending money teen-agers (particularly the suburban teen class) have at their disposal. The fact that one of our mass media —radio—plays in large measure to this market comes through loud and clear in any excursion along the kilocycles. The language of alienation and the signs of revolt among the youth stand out in book titles and in news stories in every Sunday paper.

1. What facts have special implications for the adolescent who is growing up in suburbia? One of our major characterizations of suburbia has greater immediate relevance for boys than it has for girls, but it epitomizes the issue. Dad's work is at a distance, and his worker-identity is not easily shared with his son.

Erik Erikson, a psychoanalyst who has specialized in adolescence, has described the youthful quest for *identity*. His term points to the sense of being a personal self with goals and purposes that hang together in the face of siren songs that tempt one either into regressive retreat from maturity or into such diffusion of the personal self that the ego seemingly fails to set up a boundary from the surrounding world and to say, "I am this person," and, "This is what I want to be doing." Lacking identity there will be an intense feeling of precariousness, of disunity in the self, and of inability to cope with the world.

Kenneth Keniston in *The Uncommitted,* drawing heavily upon Erikson, sees a major challenge in our technological society to be

the achievement of individual identity. In technological society every youth is confronted with a series of distant roles, organizations and institutions, each of which makes different and often conflicting demands.[4]

By contrast, in the traditional or undifferentiated community, society merely demands that men continue to be what they were born to be, and except in the case of the rebel, "fitting in" was much less a problem.

Dad and his work ought to be one source of identity for the growing boy. Work is the male's chief identity in our society. To get to know a man we often ask more readily, "What do you do?" or "Who are you with?" than to ask about his place of residence or his family lineage as older societies did. The problems of an occupation-based status system feed the particular problems faced by male youth in our culture.

Most boys once knew fairly intimately the work of their fathers, if indeed they did not actually move into exactly the same occupational pattern themselves. This was true of the farmers, shopkeepers, and early industrial workers through the nineteenth century. In the small town the son can observe his father's work at close range.

Suburbia and the technological society put a distance between children and their fathers' work. Sons are left without ready access to this source of identity with the past and this model for a possible identity in the future. Dad may be available as father and as leisure-time companion; but as wage-earner, he is something of a cipher. Thus a strong factor in growing up, identification with the parent of one's own sex, is weakened.

Because of the travel that is required of some technical, sales, and managerial personnel, many suburban fathers are absent from home for days and even weeks at a time. Daily commuting from the more distant suburbs can mean that dad leaves at dawn and returns home as younger children tumble into bed. One Y.M.C.A. worker reported that boys from the upper-middle-class suburb seem almost as seriously father-deprived as the boys from fatherless homes of the inner city.

2. The affluence of middle-class suburbia creates another

handicap to growing up with a sense of identity and competence. It tends to limit or altogether eliminate work experience from the life of the middle teen years.

The Reformers elevated work and vocation to a new level of significance in the Christian tradition. While the "Protestant ethic" presents certain difficulties today, its legacy contributed significantly to the fiber of American society. Freud himself commented on the importance of work for human well-being, and the absence of work to be done is a therapeutic hazard in the treatment of the mentally ill. Many others since Freud, in looking at the process of maturation, have stressed the essential sense of competence that comes from managing tasks which, a generation ago, the young were given to do. Sons and daughters both had regular chores in the house where there was no automatic heating system, no dishwasher, no second car for errands. They found odd jobs not only easy to obtain but necessary as sources of income for themselves or to supplement a tight family budget.

Suburban affluence has changed this. A teen-ager today has difficulty finding work, and there are fewer tasks at home. One suburban mother said, "The children these days have so much to think about and so many things to do I wouldn't dream of asking my son [a high school senior] to help with any chores at home." Paul Goodman [5] quotes a superintendent of schools in Rochester, New York: "Many parents have long since given up the struggle to encourage youths to share in the few remaining home duties that still require physical effort. Yet no school program can provide the discipline, the maturity, or the self respect that comes from performing real work that is highly valued and fairly paid for by the adult world."

Shoveling coal and earning extra cash by carrying papers

are not by any stretch of the imagination the fulfillment of adolescence. Nor, translated to the adult world, are do-it-yourself repairs on the house or successful money-making in business the fulfillment of human destiny, Christianly understood. Moreover, that high school senior did have work to do; his study in the suburban schools is challenging enough to be a vocation for the time, and it needs to be appreciated as such. (A wise state welfare commissioner proposes "paying" teen-agers from welfare families $5.00 a week to stay in school after age 16.) The tangible experience of work, however, provides both participation in the ongoing process of the family's life and contact with various people in the adult world.

Suburbia is a derivative community; it is a consumer rather than a producer. Suburban families can receive their living without much struggle and then can sit passively through TV commercials learning what more they should want with their increasing incomes. This kind of culture leaves youth short-changed and without experience of purposive activity.

3. In the newer suburbs, the adolescent has but a small functional role in community life. He feels that he has no "place." He will say he has "no place to go." High-rent shopping centers offer few soda shops, pool halls, and ice cream stores where he can hang out with his peers. Merchants keep an eye on customer turnover. Yet the adolescents are now one of the largest groups in the suburban population.

Herbert Gans generally defends suburbia against the charge that it exemplifies mass society at its worst. Suburbia serves its residents well, he says. One of the major difficulties Gans found in Levittown, however, has to do with adolescents.

> The adult conception of Levittown's vitality is not shared by its adolescents. Many consider it a dull place to which they have been brought involuntarily by their parents. Often there is no place to go and nothing to do after school.[6]

> Part of the adolescents' dissatisfaction with the community—as with adult society in general—is their functionlessness outside of school. American society really has no use for them other than as students.[7]

In short, suburban communities have not yet developed institutionalized patterns that serve teen-age needs well. The retreat to drugs for kicks is but one more symptom of the way teens experience their culture's paucity of resources in the light of their own felt personal needs.

4. One source of personal identity is the past. Keniston finds his alienated youth living for the present alone. He sees their rejection of the past and their noncommitment to any future to be in part the product of a culture that not only changes very rapidly but comes to worship change per se as good, to create built-in obsolescence in its appliances, clothing styles, and automobiles, a culture that sees even recent movies as incredibly out of date.

C. Wright Mills, in *White Collar,* argued that middle-class work and life-style lacked vitality, so the middle class has only a "history without events; whatever common interests they have do not lead to unity; whatever future they have will not be of their own making." [8]

The new suburbia, of course, has no long history. Children cannot point out the houses in which they were born; very often they no longer live in the same community or state where they did five years before. There are few landmarks, few monuments. Some developers have even removed the trees. Everything on the place is as young as the house.

Sensitive redevelopers of our cities are now urging the

retention of neighborhood landmarks and points of historical interest. As people move through a city they need help
in sensing their place in space and time. Because of its style
and newness, suburbia does too little to provide the new
generation with this kind of orientation.

5. The Christian understanding of life knows man as a
moral creature, one who experiences a claim "from outside." It sees man's fulfillment in the exercise of selfhood through intentional activity. It defines man, to use
H. R. Niebuhr's term, as the "responsible self"—man-
before-God. This intentionality is the opposite of the
cynicism that comes to say, "There is nothing given,
nothing to live *for*." Neither is it a hedonism that has
no hope: "Eat, drink, and be merry, for tomorrow—
who knows?"

If they are to be fully human, then all persons, including
youth, need a sense of reality to which they respond with intentional activity and within which they choose values for
the shaping of their lives. But today's youth, says A. H.
Maslow, an eminent psychologist, are "value-deprived."
Physical malnutrition results in scurvy or pellagra, and
there can be a similar kind of deprivation for the moral nature of man. Deprivation here results in what Maslow calls
a "metapathology."

> The metapathologies of the affluent and indulged young
> come partly from deprivation of intrinsic values, frustrated
> idealism, from disillusionment with a society they see (mis-
> takenly) motivated only by lower or animal or material
> needs. . . . To say it another way, much of the bad be-
> havior of affluent, privileged, and basic-need-gratified high
> school and college students is due to frustration of the
> idealism so often found in young people. My hypothesis is
> that this behavior can be a fusion of continued search for
> something to believe in, combined with anger at being dis-
> appointed.[9]

Paul Goodman puts it another way in a book whose main thesis is that our society does not offer opportunity enough for creative, significant, and useful work for youth *or* adults: "Our abundant society is at present simply deficient in many of the most elementary objective opportunities and worthwhile goals that could make growing up possible. . . . It is lacking in the opportunity to be useful." [10]

Even so brief an analysis provides clues for the ministry of the church with suburban youth. Ideally, the church, as a community and a "family," has a history—roots that go all the way back to the mythology of Genesis. It offers a frame of reference that can contribute to the identity of those who participate in it. As a purposive community, goal-directed in mission and service, the church can hold out for young participants a sense of direction they will not find in the life of beach parties or evenings at the drive-in and may not find even in their secular schooling. In its images of the cross, the Kingdom of Christ, and discipleship, it affords symbols through which the youth who gropes tentatively toward the largest questions of human destiny— guilt and death versus hope and meaning—may find some bedrock truth and understanding.

If alive to its own Scriptures and history, the church can talk unashamedly in terms that appeal to the idealism of youth. As in few other places people can find in the church a community institution in which families and the generations can come together. In this day when the small, isolated nuclear family unit is the suburban norm, people may find there some of the advantages the extended family system offered. Church adults can share more of themselves in a kind of vocational guidance, to supplement what little vocational contact a son or daughter can experience with one set of parents, a few neighbors, and overloaded high school guidance personnel. The church speaks of vocation in terms larger than making a living. It is a place where fathers can be seen doing more than mowing the lawn or leaving for work that is hid from view. Some churches have businessmen's committees to help teen-agers find summer employment or permanent jobs when they finish school.

The major caveat for the church is that it not sell its youth short. What is called for is less talk about "keeping *them* off the street" or "teaching *them* to go straight" and more about working together toward goals that both older and younger members of the church can share.

Youth who see adults at work in idealistic pursuits will reach partway across the generation gap themselves. That suburbanite was on the right track, plaintive as was his plea, who asked of a community organizer, "Do you think our kids would start talking to us again if we started being active on political issues?" Politics is an important supplement to discussions about making the beds and getting in on time after the Friday evening date. (One frightened mother protested a youth group program on civil rights, "There will be plenty of time for my sons to learn about problems in our society after they finish college!")

A church with meaningful programs of service to others will find youth ready to share the work. Indeed, many congregations will find themselves led by youth. One minister said quite frankly that the coffeehouse opened by the youth group was the most significant single event in the life of his congregation that whole year. In another church, a sizable youth group divided into task forces to study and then serve in half a dozen areas of community need. One group began a tutoring project, another visited in nursing homes, another found ways to help in a day care center. Before long this task-force approach became so meaningful that the adult congregation itself began to reorganize its life along the same lines, turning from a static pattern of committees and fellowship groups toward task groups for mission.

A white Southern church youth group took a weekend for study in a sharecropping black-belt community and for work alongside some of the Negro youth in refurbishing a community center. Two years later the congregation was talking about a similar field trip for adults and was developing major avenues of relationship to this mission outpost of the denomination.

As long as our society has too little "place" for adolescents, many tasks in the community go undone, tasks that the younger generation could help with as volunteers or at relatively low wages. Among the tasks are tutoring and coaching in athletic and recreational programs for children, or assistance in the work of political parties and other voluntary associations. Teen-age interest across the country was aroused and a lot of leg work was invested in campaigning for Eugene McCarthy and Robert Kennedy and, later, in raising funds for Biafran relief. Gans proposes community opinion polls and political research by teen-agers to enhance the effectiveness of suburban governments.[11]

We sell youth short when we forget that they are persons who may be ready to contribute to more formal church life itself—with music and drama and challenges to adult ideas. They may be more ready than adults to participate in corporate worship, either by sharing in its leadership as lay readers or with special contributions that make worship more the communal affair it ought to be. Youth are ready to sit on official committees and boards and in many churches they do this happily and constructively. Such administrative participation in university life is increasingly not only the demand but the pattern of youth who no longer want to share so little in the institutions of which they are a part, as if they were mere children.

Taking youth seriously involves a conscious recognition of teen problems and teen culture. One Detroit church in the inner city recognizes the distinctiveness of a younger group by providing monthly services in a "Teen and Twenty Chapel." More and more suburban churches are sponsoring occasional services of worship in the verbal and musical idiom of youth culture. It is helpful if adults make serious attempts to participate with youth in worship by periodic use of such resources in the major programs and services of the congregation. Frank discussion of the generation gap is appropriate. A California church held a seminar on "pop" music for adults who want to understand teen-agers. Homework assignment: "Listen to your children's records."

Taking youth seriously suggests congregational recognition of events important in young lives. If marriages and hospitalizations are mentioned in church newsletters, high school graduations should be too. One Dallas church has celebrated the "Feast of Coming of Age." The pastor proposes other feasts as well, among them the "Feast of the Driver's Licence." [12] Another minister, taking a cue from Erikson's "eight stages of man" wonders whether the church needs more "rites of passage" to supplement those the church already has in Baptism, confirmation, marriage, and the patterns surrounding serious illness, death, and bereavement. Such an approach at least suggests latent meanings in programs we dismiss all too lightly—the kindergarten tableaux, the Girl Scout Sundays, God and country ceremonies, the gift of the Bible at fourth-grade levels, and First Communion, an important Catholic tradition. These ceremonials in church life lay the groundwork for teen participation in the church if the break with childhood patterns that is appropriate to the teen years is fully acknowledged.

The suburban church that wants an effective ministry with the youth of its community will have to recognize the staff needs that such ministry implies. Volunteers or professionals are needed to spend time with adolescents in these purposive endeavors. Cooperative support for the minister who wants to give his time to youth leadership—such as a fortnight, in the summer, for directing camps and conferences—is a part of the congregation's contribution. Hiring for part-time work a public school teacher who has the knack of being able to work with teen groups and who can train and coordinate the work of volunteers is an opportunity for the smaller church.

Some will ask: "What has all this social service to do with the church? The church should bring youth into membership and teach them Christian faith." These terms need reworking because they are static. To a go-go generation they have too little challenge. Put it another way, and we may be saying much the same thing: The church is charged to share with youth *its life of mission*.

Many significant programs of church youth appear to have relatively little to say about Christianity per se. But if they are an integral part of congregational life that includes worship and study as more explicit expressions of faith, the programs are more meaningful to youth today than the old patterns of Christian Endeavor. Doctrinal lines become very fluid in these servant enterprises; many "Protestant" groups have Roman Catholic and Jewish members. "Religion" takes on very broad and sometimes bizarre meanings in teen-age bull sessions, but theological naïveté is not limited to youth. If today's youth activities provide church contacts that involve trust of adults, meaningful service in the world, and an accepting peer group, they are part of a total development of identity. Such a process mediates basic ingredients of Christian faith and life.

Many concerns are necessarily bypassed in sketching one perspective on youth. Nothing has been said here about sex, drugs, light shows, intimacy needs, motivation for college, or contemporary music in youth culture. These issues will find their place when we take youth seriously as creative, growing, moral beings instead of treating them like children. If taken seriously, and if he realizes purposes in life broader than private hedonism, the adolescent will have less need to get his kicks from drugs. Growing toward purposive maturity, a youth will have enough self-respect and concern for others that he will not fall into sexual promiscuity.

Such a perspective on youth throws us back upon the adult society in which their lives are set. If youth is "value-deprived," the adult world that nurtures them is under judgment. Some further words from Keniston serve well as a summary:

> American society makes extraordinary demands on its members—that they adapt to chronic social change, that they achieve a sense of personal wholeness in a complex and fragmented society, that they resolve major discontinuities between childhood and adulthood, and that they locate positive values in an intellectual climate which consistently undermines such values.[18]

Granted the major cultural dilemmas represented in those phrases, the church has its work cut out for it in work with youth, particularly, perhaps, the middle-class youth of suburbia.

2. MARY BROWNING: FIFTH WHEEL AT THIRTY-FIVE?

Mary Browning sat down for a second cup of coffee. She looked from the kitchen window into a cloudy, gray day. Jack had left for work nearly two hours ago; three children were more or less happily off to school. Mary had yet to get dressed and finish cleaning up the kitchen.

"Today," she was musing, "I must not spend so much time on the phone with Debby. I should plant the tulip bulbs for next spring, make some plans for Christmas gifts, consider having a dinner party one of these weekends before they all slip by, write to mother and to Jack's folks, see if there is a piano teacher whom we could afford for Martha sometime after the first of the year. And I must vacuum the rooms I didn't finish yesterday. I think I will tear into all of this and then stop after lunch and start a good book.

"But will I? I said exactly the same thing six weeks ago and I haven't yet even picked out the book. Why don't I get anything accomplished?

"What's Jack doing now? At least he's with other people. He is probably enjoying himself at work. Travel on this new assignment next week will be good for him. I wonder if I could go with him some of the time when the children are older.

"I used to complain about baby talk all day, but it's lonely in this house when all the children are in school. At first I looked forward to the peace and quiet, but it's getting old. I was never isolated like this when we were in the city. There isn't even a corner store within walking distance out here. It's too chilly for any of the neighbors to be outside today. Maybe Debby would come over for coffee later.

"What would it be like to be working? The middle hours of the day drag on so, now they have the cafeteria at school. What was the ad I saw? 'Make money in your own home— a hundred plans for money-making homework. $3.95!' Do you suppose one day I could write children's books or open a little gift shop somewhere? Maybe TV would cheer me up."

Mary Browning has in mind a list of chores so long she often feels interrupted as well as relieved in the afternoon when the children return. She is also uninspired by the chores, and that is why they have not been done. At thirty-five she is beginning to feel like a fifth wheel and when she is forty it will be worse. Some would say that Mary was not loved enough in her childhood to have a sense of her own worth in the present. Others, however, could say she has enough sense of her own worth to be dissatisfied with a suburban social structure that does not put her talents to good use.

Judging from their use of psychiatrists, barbiturates, and tranquilizers, the women of suburbia are no happier than their adolescent children or their husbands. Books by both men and women convey the impression that many of these women are, in fact, seriously dissatisfied with their apparently wholesome suburban destiny. Spectorsky reports a doctor's comments, referring to women who suffer psychogenic abortions at midpregnancy, on the "unhappiness which is at the core of their lives." [14] Novelists portray a frantic search by women in our culture—through sex, through having children, through being free from children, through religious ritual—for a peace that eludes them.

Mary Ellman, in *Thinking About Women,* finds a consistently patronizing and often hostile attitude toward women reflected in general literature right down to the present. In *The Feminine Mystique,* Betty Friedan complains that the myth of femininity is a balloon in need of puncture. According to the myth, women can be fulfilled in living out what our culture holds up as the feminine image—mothers, homemakers, attractive mistresses for their mates.

Few types of articles appear more regularly in the women's magazines than those which present in glowing terms a once-drab room redone in red and gold, a new way for living within a budget, for disciplining the children, or renewing a waning marital glow. There is nothing wrong with these simple suggestions except that they speak in tones that seem to offer salvation from existential despair. Mary Browning has tried them, and she begins to doubt.

Of course there are millions of healthy, happy suburban women. But there are also any number suffering such deep frustrations that unhappiness of a sort is indeed at the core of their lives.

The job description of the housewife does not inspire Mary Browning. Take the matter of transportation. Distance in suburbia adds on hours of time to this particular chore. Research reports suggest that on the average, the "American woman" spends only 2 of the 99.6 hours of her work week at the task of driving. Mary Browning will tell you, however, that in suburbia the figure can mount to fifteen and more, if she drives Jack to the train, takes children into the city to the museum, to the doctor, to the movies, or to dancing lessons, or if she drives around much in the sprawling suburb itself. Providing transportation is her next most time-consuming activity after housework, and its satisfactions wear very thin.

Frustrated anger on the job is not born from the chore in itself, however. Unhappiness derives from seeing little purpose in the chores or from expectations that there should be more satisfaction than there is. Those women's magazines with their suggestions on color schemes, budgets, discipline problems, and marital relations are legitimate "professional journals" for the homemaker *if* the vocation of housewife and chauffeur and husband-tender is seen as meaningful. Our culture and Mary's propensities do not make that role meaningful enough, however, to satisfy her and many of her peers.

One part of the reason is to be found in the culture's habit of measuring a person's worth by his paycheck. The press occasionally attempts to do housewives a good turn by defending them in terms of dollars and cents, but in doing so it only compounds the problem. (Distributing those 99.6 hours to various skills they represent—nursemaid at $1.25 an hour, cook at $2.50, etc.—the housewife is told she is "worth" $8,285.68 a year.[15]) In a society that measures nearly everything in monetary terms, Mary Browning gets no paycheck.

Then there is the matter of isolation. Mary can easily succumb to a sense of being left out, a feeling reinforced by a contrast of her work with that of the husband, by the derivative and satellite status of the suburb, and by the spread of tract housing on half-acre lots that leaves Mary with the children and little else till Jack comes home from town.

Many women in suburbia have been educated to competence and expectations that also help prevent the housewife role from offering fulfillment. Increasingly the wives of suburbia are a college-trained group of women, trained not as housewives but as persons in their own right with varied avocational interests and specialized competences. These women may have found satisfactions before marriage in the exercise of these capabilities. Yet the early years of marriage usually require that they be full-time mothers and homemakers, receiving their sense of meaning vicariously through their childern and their husbands' worth.

One scholar summarizes the culture's picture of this suburban wife and her vocation in the following way:

> Among the implied functions of the family—and of the wife as its manager—are to send the husband off to work in a "good mood" and have a cheerful and relaxing reception awaiting when he returns exhausted and full of pent up feelings after a "hard day's work." Implicitly, then, work leads to the accumulation of "bad" feelings accumulated on the job. The wife is the "mood manager" of her family: she must sense the husband's moods, encourage him to talk about his problems with her, follow his work enough so that she can understand these problems, keep the house, the children, and above all herself relaxed and attractive, be warm, open, responsive, attentive, and never tired or bored. That part of a woman's life that is not taken up with her children, should, according to exhortations of the mass media, be devoted to anticipating and dealing with the feelings of her husband. . . . Only bad wives go out with the girls when husbands are home.[16]

Mary Browning finally begins to feel that this is a sophisticated kind of slavery, this vicarious definition of meaning to her life and work.

What shall we define as a woman's needs and as the possible contribution by the church in the light of this set of culture-bred tensions? Obviously one of the first needs is a deeper societal acceptance of women as persons no more expected to find their satisfactions merely through the lives and accomplishments of others than any other class of people. That is what feminist movements are really all about. This does not necessitate the end of feminine sexuality, nor of assumptions that there are differences in the roles of men and women. It does not imply that the Kingdom will have arrived in some distant day when corporate executives and attorneys and senators and cabdrivers are equally men and women. It does imply the increasing acceptance of women as equals in the work world, well beyond what is the case at present, as well as due credit for the avocational pursuits of women who do not work.

With machines doing heavy labor, the faulty arguments about the weaker sex have little relevance. Women live longer than men and can be described as the stronger sex, as Ashley Montagu has done in *The Natural Superiority of Women*. Nonetheless, without adopting Victorian models for womanhood, we can rationally project continuing differences in style for men and women in the home and outside at work. The bearing of children and the care of the newborn is one obvious case in which a woman's role is laid out for her by nature, and one that inevitably influences her pattern of life during the childbearing years. Nearly all developmental treatments of children put heavy emphasis on the early infant-mother relationship. In theory, doubtless, this "mother" could be a father or a nursemaid, but the natural mother is almost always the one with this profoundly significant function.

Psychoanalytic insights into sexual correlations with temperament and life-style allow us a further kind of speculation as to the different contributions of men and women in society.[17] The psychoanalytic interpreter would say the male is likely to be more aggressive and competitive, more "instrusive." The woman is more likely to express her sense of the world and her selfhood in receptive, nurturing, and enveloping activity, incorporating and softening masculine aggressiveness. It would not be altogether unexpected, therefore, if, as American women go increasingly to work, they more often become doctors and less often space pilots, more often teachers and less often miners, more often architects and less often demolition experts, more often diplomats and less often army generals. Clearly, as we put down such speculations we are making two points. First, we do not tell the woman her permanent place is that of mother and homemaker alone. The father has a very important place as "family man" and homemaker too; the woman has other avenues of self-fulfillment and service open to her. Secondly, this way of describing a temperamental difference between the sexes means that in the social process itself there are complementary relationships that make the "feminine" characteristics extremely important, important even to our human survival in this nuclear age. We can look forward to increased sharing of leadership between men and women in public life and the work world as well as in the home.[18]

We must return, however, to Mary Browning, the Mary Browning with a junior college education, three years' experience as a secretary, and then the children and that house in Cloverdale, or the Mary Browning with a four-year bachelors' degree and two years' experience as a teacher before Cloverdale and a lawyer husband. Mary Browning can be expected to be normally happy for a few years *if:* if she hasn't in her own mind reluctantly given up a career for the sake of a husband and then a pregnancy, if she has had a childhood with other children and therefore has not only a sense of the profound significance of mothering but some self-confidence in that sometimes frightening, often frustrating, tedious new job, and if she has a husband who is in this *with* her as a father as well as a breadwinner.

In these childbearing years there is a good chance that Mary will be happier than most people most of the time, for in the entire bodily-spiritual economy of the race there are few moments that offer such clear-cut clues to identity and purpose as this generative stage of mothering. It is not surprising that Christian Baptism, early in church history, included the children in the households of converts and then came to be administered to the newborn infant. Birth and mothering are too significant not to be recognized and celebrated by the community of faith. It is not surprising that legend and poetry carved out a significant place for Mary in the Gospels, or that the madonna has such a place in Christian art. This imagery can serve to express for the new mother something of the ultimate significance that she has a right to experience, a significance undergirding such thoroughly mundane assignments as changing diapers and surviving nights of colic.

A good chance, yes; but Mary may not be happy even in these years, and a church concerned for people (and infants' need of happy mothers) does well to take account of reasons why she may not be. One of the major reasons lies in the nuclear family structure of our society. Again the social scientist:

> Sociological isolation of the family entails the psychological isolation of the woman in charge of the family. The isolation is especially telling when it comes to raising children. Many American women have little prior knowledge of children . . . [and] great uncertainty about how to raise their own . . . even about how to "be" with them. . . . Dr. Spock is not an adequate substitute for the experience of living with children and being helped by those who know them. The easy passage of lore about children from one generation to the next, in a community where children are always underfoot and are everyone's

responsibility, has completely disappeared from middle-class American life; and the substitutes do not fill the emotional gap.[19]

Mothering instinct itself normally makes for anxiety about the welfare of newborn children, the proximity of good medical facilities notwithstanding. Add to that the emotional uncertainties born of inexperience, and the sudden shift from courtship, higher education, or part-time work to the confinement of caring for the first child. The young-mother syndrome is understandable. A major task of every couple is that of being parents, an important role in life for which they are relatively untrained. Unspecialized by age group, in touch as it is with family units across the generation gap, the church can foster responsible reflection upon the vocation of parenthood.

When Mary Browning finally sends her last child off to kindergarten she looks into a thousand mornings and wonders about meaning beyond what she found in giving birth to babies, even beyond getting teen-agers ready for college. Will vicarious satisfaction in Jack's achievements and in growing children be enough?

At this stage Mary may begin to think of culture. She redecorates the house, enrolls in a mail-order course on art appreciation, attends an extension course in ceramics, takes up tennis, or gets out the flute she played in the college orchestra and dreams of a woodwind ensemble. Jack goes along with all this, tolerant, a little puzzled and a little bit amused—just as Mary patiently looks upon some thing Jack himself takes so seriously as "good recreation, time profitably spent"—his workshop equipment (far too expensive to be justified by anything he ever built) and his golfing. She may seek out companionship in a bowling group, a book club, a women's circle at the church. Nonetheless as time wears on, she may still experience profound frustration because time does not hang together for her.

Neither the culture as it is nor any dictionary of Christian practice has ready answers for Mary Browning. Mary may find considerable satisfaction in her cultural activity —her music or painting or poetry. Beauty has always been a meaning-yielding pursuit for both philosophers and more ordinary mortals, a vehicle for glorifying God, for finding the human situation rich and full.

Mary may find in the give-and-take with good companions, particularly if she and Jack are with other couples in small and intimate groups—reading, bowling, swimming, or just plain bridge—the kind of human relationship that sustains her.

But she may not. A writer in quite another field, industrial relations, suggests that there are not one set of values to be attended to in building satisfaction at the job, but two. One is what he calls "hygiene," the usual concern for working conditions—wages, safety, noise level. But at best, all that can be achieved on this scale is a lack of dissatisfaction, not a positive pleasure in the job. On quite another scale, positive satisfaction is a possibility. Here the means toward satisfaction are not elements of "hygiene," but elements of purpose—the opportunity for creative investment of the self in the work, the purposeful teaming up with fellow workers, the inner sense of what it is all about.

Discussing the "mom" stereotype that in the late '40s was blamed for many sons who were psychiatric rejects from the draft, Erik Erikson wrote of the "middle range of mature womanhood" that was crowded out from these women's lives. " 'Mom' is a woman in whose life cycle remnants of infantility join advanced senility to crowd out the middle range of mature womanhood, which thus becomes self-absorbed and stagnant. In fact she mistrusts her own feelings as a woman and mother. . . . This 'mom' is not happy; she does not like herself; she is ridden with anxiety that her life was a waste . . . a victim, not a victor." [20]

Mary Browning asks not only "hygiene" in her life, but purpose. She seeks expression in mature womanhood that will prevent self-absorption and stagnation. With her life she wants to do something she sees as meaningful, something that fits into purposes that transcend her own mere physical survival. She has the time and the kind of self-esteem that asks for a chance to invest herself in more ways than writing letters to her children off at college and in keeping house for Jack.

The church need not necessarily enter at this point. However, even if Mary Browning finds a "secular" solution to her frustrations, she is asking a religious question. She is asking for a pattern of living that makes her life significant, a sense of context that finally includes even the largest issues—life, death, hope, despair. The religious community attempts to mediate to its surrounding culture just such a pattern of living and such a sense of context.

Mary may find much of what she is hunting for in one of two directions: she may move into the "career" of work in the voluntary associations or she may go to work. We briefly consider each of these alternatives.

If Mary moves into activity with the League of Women Voters, the P.T.A., the Junior League, the A.A.U.W., or a human relations organization, or if she works with a political party, the auxiliary at the hospital, or one of the United Fund organizations, she may be teased by a few men as a "clubwoman" or a "do-gooder." She has a right, however, to be recognized as a woman who has found a part-time activity that contributes to the coherence and humanity of her society and that has considerable potential for doing more. By virtue of the activities of women like Mary Browning, everything from day nurseries to revisions in town charters are launched and manage to succeed. Agglomerations of people become communities as a result. That women perform in civic work "careers" with a style that is their own, and do it in large measure because they enjoy the process, is only to say of them what we can also say of men at their middle-class occupations. What the morally alert woman and the concerned church group can do is forward the critical and evaluative processes that channel the nearly incredible energies available for this kind of activity in the most constructive directions possible.

If Mary goes to work, she no longer faces the raised eyebrows she would have faced a generation or two ago. If she earns at a rate somewhat equivalent to that of her husband, there may be some adjustments to make in her marriage. In their own minds men normally "wear the pants" because they bring home the paycheck. If she isn't sure about working, Mary can rationalize by saying that she needs the money. In absolute terms she does not, but in an emotional sense she may, for money reassures her about the value of what she does.

If "total labor force" adds up to the well-being of the populace, we can assume that the job Mary takes on will make some contribution beyond the satisfactions she herself derives, but those satisfactions are significant in themselves. The job gets Mary into the swim of things, contributes something to her sense of identity and purpose, provides a role beyond that of "housewife." Moreover, because Jack is already breadwinner, Mary can take less into account the financial return from her work. She may choose to work where the present economy does not provide much in the way of income incentives. She may elect to work with children, for example, to enter social work, to serve with the church or social agencies.

Because of her own self-image as a homemaker as well as a worker, Mary will find it ideal to work part time. If business and industry were to structure more part-time jobs during school hours, after the pattern of many informal agencies and businesses, a ready pool of creative talent would be available and many a woman would find an outlet for energies that are now unused.

If we now look at the church's relation to Mary Browning, we must first acknowledge two facts: (1) Mary's mother and grandmother had many of the same needs that Mary has and they met those needs through "church work" —sewing circles, home missions groups, Ladies Aid societies, fund-raising bazaars. (2) These patterns, meaningful once, are often inappropriate today. They do not satisfy Mary. They sell short her training and talents. In their impact on society they often distort her intentions and the intentions that the church should have in worldly ministry. They squander her time in petty money-making activities. They use a Band-aid approach to human misery and injustice instead of seeking out the causes of social injury. Many a Mary Browning is alert enough to comprehend all of this and is eager for a new approach. When she is faced with a choice of putting in time on a church committee to help the junior choir, or strengthening an integrated P.T.A., or sharpening her own skills as a social worker, traditional church work comes in a very poor third.

For every woman who feels at home with present pat-

terns of church activity, there is one who does not, one who
is highly motivated nonetheless to be of service in the community and who is affirmative in her outlook on religion.
With a radiant smile, a pleasant white suburban woman in
her late fifties summed up the difference one day in 1965:
"Some of us who never dreamed of walking in a picket
line joined the March on Washington in 1963. Our lives
haven't been the same since then." The suburban congregation of the last third of the twentieth century must take
a new look at Mary Browning in several ways.

1. For one thing, Mary may not be particularly competent as a lay theologian and she may be Biblically illiter-
ate, but she has enough education so that the church can
no longer talk down to her with canned devotionals at
women's meetings and with speakers who have merely a
sentimental concern for the faith and the world. Jesus at
the home of Martha and Mary commended Mary as the
one who had chosen the better part, that which would not
be taken away from her, in contrast to the troubled house-
keeping of Martha. (Luke 10:38-42.) We may legitimately
read this as an emphasis upon the need for reflection in full
human life; we may note in its domestic setting the impli-
cation that homemakers are people with minds and hearts
as well as hands. Mary Browning may be ready for serious
reading in a study group among her peers or in couples
groups that are vehicles for both fellowship and learning.
If some men now need to be retrained for their changing
work three times in a lifetime, Mary Browning needs opportunities to keep on learning too.

Abraham Maslow, who was mentioned above in connec-
tion with his comments on youth, describes "the desire to
know and understand" as a human need every bit as real
as more commonly acknowledged needs like rest and food,

one that comes into play when the more basic needs are met. "I have seen many women," he says, "intelligent, prosperous, and unoccupied, slowly develop . . . symptoms of intellectual inaction." Maslow says that they develop the same symptoms as some men who are confined to meaningless work—loss of zest in life, self-dislike, general depression of bodily functions, symptoms "produced in intelligent people leading stupid lives in stupid jobs." [21] Study may play a role in keeping Mary Browning happy and more fully alive.

Churches must be alert to the intellectual sophistication in suburban populations. One Rhode Island church employed as coequal to its preaching pastor a Ph.D. who was education minister for adults.[22] He organized intensive college-level courses of study for people from the congregation and the wider suburban community, text books, tuition fees, and all. The continuing education of adults in our society is one of the mushrooming and highly significant sectors of the "knowledge industry." Suburban churches can expect to play a part in this development.

2. The alert church will be prepared to act as a broker or middleman, helping Mary Browning find meaningful use for her time and talents. It matters little whether this activity is within or outside church structures. If Mary's "career" is on the volunteer side and she serves in a human relations council of the suburb or a child care center in the city, Mary's church will applaud her even if it means that Mary will refuse to take on a church committee assignment. Mary will be an added interpreter of human rights or poverty within the congregation and an agent to help other Mary Brownings find the satisfaction of meaningful voluntary work.

3. The church itself will seek more meaningful activities

for women, if it does not abolish separate women's activities altogether. A group of younger women, for example, may gather not around the typical "circle" program but around concern for education, equipping themselves with some insight into educational theory and relating this interest to the quality of schools in the suburb and in the city. Some members may affiliate with outside action groups in education and press for reforms at the state or federal level.[23]

Committees and task groups with social action interests will capitalize on a woman's time and initiative for civic concerns. They may assign research to women who will represent the church at such meetings as the town school board or metropolitan church mission groups and on community programs dealing with housing or race. Feedback from these meetings will always be sought for the task groups or action committees and then frequently forwarded in some way to the congregation at large.

4. The congregation will look to its own internal polity to prevent the segregation by sexes that leaves women in religious purdah—women's work, kitchen duties and house committees, but never in positions on the diaconate (consistory, vestry), the board of trustees, or pastoral supply committee. Such segregation acquiesces to the cultural bias against women, and it denies those particular insights which women may have to offer in the broader work of the church.

5. Women, by virtue of their presence in suburbia more of the time than men, are likely to be in touch with one another through a surprisingly efficient informal communications network. Women are able to serve remarkably as propagandists for a new idea. Quiet work among liberal white women in the South has helped influence many a

male decision maker. Friendly Town exchanges (inner-city children visiting for a vacation in a suburban or rural community) have been promoted through casual woman-to-woman talk over backyard fences. The natural sympathies of activist women, once sensitized and informed, should form a strong suburban truth squad to educate a community on the need for a better health and welfare program for inner-city mothers, housing code enforcement on slum landlords, aid for inner-city schools and United Fund agencies. Women can make (or break) an open-enrollment scheme, designed to combat racial imbalance in the schools of a suburban town, or a program for bussing city Negro children to the suburbs for schooling. An organized network of committed women is a useful instrument for any church or secular group ready to move on an issue. Person-to-person communication holds a movement together as can nothing else in a day of too much "junk mail" and simple newsletter duplication.

6. It is common knowledge that women make decisions governing the disposal of more consumer dollars than do men. Therefore, stewardship interpretation and patterns of giving are not matters for men only. If Mary Browning works, she can participate even more easily through financial aid in her political party, civil rights groups, the United Fund, and church mission projects. Money, in an affluent society, is one of the readiest means through which busy people who live at a distance in the suburbs can participate in urban social change.

If churches adopt a more incisive program for women, "women's work" may in the future attract the Mary Brownings who now find activities elsewhere much more attractive, activities with a less significant potential for community welfare. The church does not have to be converted into a human relations council or a political party to in-

clude action as a major part of its total celebration and
service in the world. As a fellowship of those who care for
each other and who engage to care about the world around
them, all in the same name of a caring God, it will help the
Mary Brownings find significance in the second half of life,
a period that can otherwise seem all too peripheral in the
vital, pulsing, metropolitan life of the twentieth century.

3. Men at Work

Metropolitan geography splits Jack Browning's life in
half; it separates the work world from the home world.
Jack lives out many roles—husband, father, citizen, neighbor, church participant; but as important to him as any of
these, and possibly outranking them all, is his work. It is
usually in his work that a man asserts his energies of mind
or skill most effectively. It is here that he contributes to
the economic fabric of the social order. Yet, ironically, the
moral world to Jack Browning and his fellow suburbanites
is likely to be seen as the home world. The other world?
"Well, business is business." Nonetheless, underneath it
all, such a moral split troubles Jack and his friends.

Work place and home were joined in rural society.
("Bringing in the Sheaves," they sang in church.) The two
worlds were joined in cottage industry and in the city shops
when the family lived up above the store. In early industrial cities, the worker lived in the shadow of his factory.

Suburbanization has meant moving home and work
place apart from each other across the metropolis. Hence
the alienation of the work world from the moral life becomes one of the most obvious points at which to reflect on
the life of the suburban male and the church's ministry in
his world.

Despite Jack Browning's feeling that religious and moral

concerns center in the more private world of family and home and leisure time, an array of moral issues is implicit in his work, whether he is foreman, engineer, or vice president for a corporation, whether he is a professional or a businessman. The issues leap far beyond the question of finding personal meaning at work to those of justice in the social order. They have to do with promise-keeping in the commitments between corporate groups of men, with structural arrangements whose actual results are exploitation of one group of men by another, with corporate irresponsibility to future generations, and with such idolization of economic values that other cultural goals are eclipsed. Important questions may go unanswered because of systemic inertia ("It's always been our practice . . .") or because, on facing them, other values are more important ("Were we to honor that agreement to the letter, we would go bankrupt") ; but they also go unanswered simply for lack of a critical moral concern within the work world.

Sample the issues that beg a moral reflection that is deeper than a glib business-is-business mentality. (1) A public relations man puzzles over his responsibilities as advocate. Must he present his client's image to the public in the best possible light even when he is asked to distort the truth? What does a "professional" owe the public good? (2) An industrialist, involved in economic development overseas, runs up against impossible obstacles until he succumbs to bribery, confirming what he reads in his business magazine: "In almost every country throughout the underdeveloped world, a businessman can buy protection and grease the skids for a successful negotiation. . . . Probably no aspect of dealing with investment problems in the underdeveloped countries is more disturbing to Americans than the matter of graft. . . . How should one prepare to deal with graft? . . . In countries where payoff is as much a part of economic process as payroll, whose ethical standards are right, the visitors' or the natives'? Is management's role that of developer of wealth *and* missionary simultaneously, or is it true that better standards of living are prerequisites to 'better' ethics." [24] (3) A personnel manager finds irrefutable evidence that one of his district sales managers patterns his "outside" life in a way that can only be described as promiscuous. Discharging the employee and rationalizing about some possible reflection on the company, he nonetheless wonders how far he has a right to let his own standards of virtue influence his decisions about hiring and firing. (4) A machinist (and union officer) realizes that a resistant employer has become legalistic about contract rules, too careless with the safety of workers, too harsh in an efficiency campaign, and unfair to union spokesmen in the work force. The boss has also been contracting out work in a petty effort to avoid overtime pay. Therefore the employee understands the men who have taken out their hostility in sabotage. Nonetheless, to him it is wrong and he wonders about his responsibilities in the plant and to the union.

These men define their problems in personal terms, but the dilemmas can also be presented in structural language. What is a professional definition of responsibilities in public relations work? What is the function of the foreign investor and developer? What is the nature of personal privacy and freedom over against the job and the employer? What are the responsibilities of political leadership in a harrassed labor union? Putting the issues in the language of institutions, instead of personal ethics, demonstrates that most of these problems can be tackled adequately only by the serious concern of groups of men and the evolutionary processes that generate moral norms for conduct in the collectives of the work world. There are few easy answers to such dilemmas, for, as with most serious ethical questions, competing sets of values are involved. It may be a matter of going under or of maintaining employment by a (slight?) compromise of principle. It may be a choice between raising the standards of living for an overseas population by virtue of investment or of staying honest (making less money?) and not going in at all. It may be the problem of keeping peace in the union *or* democracy, but not both and perhaps neither.

One legitimate way to meet the moral dilemmas of the job is to change work and invest one's life in an institution more self-consciously dedicated to the welfare of others than are most economic enterprises. A chemist, wishing to do more significant work than he sees in industry, saves and borrows for a master's degree in social work and then takes a position with a social agency. An insurance salesman moves into business management for an educational institution. A lawyer for an international banking firm, unhappy with arranging loans that simply transfer money from one place to another, each time at a higher rate of interest, until the underdeveloped country where his heart is pays to affluent Americans at three times the prime rate at home, leaves the firm and attaches himself as an attorney to an organization promoting housing for low-income groups. ("The work was killing a part of me," he said, "and I think it was killing others.")

In each of these cases there is little question about the contribution made by the individual in his new position. Erik Erikson, to whom we referred earlier, describes the major crisis in the adult stage of life as an option between generativity and self-absorption. Suburban parents meet much of this need by providing a good life to children, and by pursuits of their own creative hobbies, but they also hunger for meaningful avenues of service beyond the family. That man is fortunate who has talent and spirit enough to make such a change as these men did and to fulfill his generativity needs so explicitly in a change of work. It is a tragic commentary upon the work world that many men see little possibility for interpreting the work they do as a generous service of the public good unless they engage in dishonest rationalizing.

To universalize the step these men took is out of the question, however. For one thing, the problems of greed, mediocrity, backbiting, and institutional self-aggrandizement are jut as pervasive and sometimes more insidious in fields such as education, social service, and organized religion. (A college catalog once advertised that its location was "seven miles from sin," but there is no such place.) Moreover the decisions these men made do little for the chemical industry, insurance business, and banking, and these enterprises are also functional parts of contemporary society.

The alternative is to stay with the work and struggle with the moral questions there. What is Jack Browning's moral style as he "hangs in there" at his work? What are his goals beyond support for his family and the satisfaction of participating in the productive process? Fundamentally Jack is called to be free enough to entertain ideas of institutional change in his work situation. If Jack Browning is to remain a moral being while pursuing his occupational routine, he must be free enough to recognize that he does not live by his job and its ideologies alone. This recognition is an echo of the kind of radical religious freedom expressed in Luther's hymn, "A Mighty Fortress Is Our God," when he says, "Let goods and kindred go." Jack must know, as Jesus said, that "the sabbath was made for man, not man for the sabbath." Putting it in contemporary terms, the Institution or the System is made for man and not man for the Institution. False idols in the work place are to be challenged as they are anywhere else. "Economic man," for example, who is thought always to struggle in order to maximize profits and to compete at the expense of his neighbor, is a myth. Human motivation is far more complex, and more redeemable. The acquisitiveness of modern business is partly institutional; far too often the socially taught criterion for business decisions is simply to make money, even if this conflicts with the common good. One part of a Christian's vocation is to work at modifying such built-in assumptions about values in business enterprise.

Keniston's uncommitted youth completed the sentence, "Most work in America is . . ." with terms such as "a rat race," "unrelieved routine," "monotonous." [25] Most work will meet those very expectations unless it is saved by some distancing of the moral self from the pressures and routines of the job. If our system leaves pockets of poverty in the affluent society ("The stingiest welfare state in the Western world," Michael Harrington called it), creates racist resentments, leaves the Third World hungry, and biases foreign policy toward simplistic military solutions, that system, like the Sabbath, begs questioning. Our nation, as we say when we pledge allegiance, is "under God."

In short, Jack Browning needs a religious perspective on his work. He needs to know that his work and the system stand under judgment and that institutional change at his work can be one manifestation of "redemption," a process in which he is called to participate. No group of people has more potential significance for enriching our common life, given this understanding, than the men of suburbia. These men of the technostructure possess skills in social organization and in economic productivity which can be used to build a more just society. In the American society this new class is becoming the dominant new "proletariat." Considering the advances in electronic control of information and production, it is not difficult to imagine men of this proletariat becoming cogs within a vast computerized machine, subject to the system instead of its masters. But moral man has another vocation. The vast information system can serve man as well as enslave him. These men of the technostructure establish the character of all the "little governments" that rule our lives—the corporations, some of which are more powerful than most state and municipal governments. These men need to learn to ride herd on the system for the sake of human goals.

It is no easy task. John Galbraith describes the subtle ease with which not only the members of the technostructure but the culture at large may fall victim to its own ideologies and lose the margin of detachment by means of which to make human judgments on the system:

> It is the genius of the industrial system that it makes the goals that reflect its needs—efficient production of goods, a steady expansion in their consumption, a powerful preference for goods over leisure, an unqualified commitment to technological change, autonomy for the technostructure, an adequate supply of trained and educated manpower—coordinate with social virtue and human enlightenment. These goals are not thought to be derived from our environment. They are assumed to be original with human personality.

The compelling need, says Galbraith, is "to have clearly in view, the dimensions of life which the industrial system, by its nature does not or cannot serve and which, because of its disabilities, it will tend to minimize." [26]

The religious man, even while working within the technostructure, must be able to challenge its priorities. He should be able to understand the genesis of the college generation's suspicions about the "Establishment." One businessman saw a student lapel button, "We're only number three and we don't give a damn." In a church discussion group he revealed his own entrapment in the system by saying, "I don't understand a person like that, a person who doesn't want to be top man."

Just how far the fascinating and seductive system of the work world can carry us is well illustrated by a comment of one researcher of the technostructure, in this case a high-up member of the scientific community. Writing in *The New Brahmins,* Spencer Klaw quotes Nobel physicist I. I. Rabi. Rabi was contemplating a possible resurgence of the arts and was musing about what would happen if "we were to become a nation of poets and were taught in school, as the Japanese are taught, that every good citizen should write a poem." He continued: "Some [poems] would be very good, and people would read and enjoy them, but what would anybody talk about? Only everyday things—love, sorrow, life, and death. If men want to go beyond these everyday things to a grand theme, they will find it only in science." [27] The Christian happens to believe that "everyday things," in fact, test the ultimate significance of Rabi's "grand theme" of science, the industrialist's visions of bigger and best, and the idealogue's myths of the market system and free enterprise.

A sharp contrast with these comments appears in the words of Lord Keynes, the brilliant British financier and economist, a man who had equal warrant for becoming preoccupied with his own science, but one who did not. Keynes said his chief hope was for the day "when the Economic Problem will take the back seat where it belongs, and the arena of the heart and head will be occupied, or reoccupied, by our real problems—the problems of life and of human relations, of creation and behavior and religion." [28]

Does the suburban church have anything to do with all of this? The stark contrast between the two images—the competitive "rat race" of work on the one hand and "Mary and the kids" on the other—itself demonstrates the difficulties confronting the suburban church when it attempts to help Jack Browning articulate concern for this area of societal life. Nonetheless, churches, because they see a man's life as a moral unity, are called to bring the work world within the orbit of religious reflection and action.

1. Within the life of the congregation there are various ways that explicit attempts to bridge the split between the work world and the home world may be made. One of the more striking attempts of this sort is recorded in a book called *The 7:05 and the Church Alive*.[29] A church at Chappaqua, New York, for several years each autumn arranged for a separate rail coach on the commuter train into Grand Central Terminal. In the coach seventy participants joined in seminars on religious ethics in business eight Mondays in succession. A public-address system was installed and seats were set back to back for discussion by foursomes throughout the coach. "Opening statements end by North White Plains, discussion begins at Pleasantville," ran one newspaper account. "Shortest sixty-five-minute ride I've ever had on this train," was a typical reaction. The content was important, but so too was the symbolism of the series, a

reflective process linking suburb and the work place. "Do you have love for a man who has blocked your job progress and your income and your security?" "How do you deal with a boss who instructs his employees to exaggerate expense statements as a means of raising their pay and evading taxes?" These were sample questions from the suggestion box.

There are other ways to grapple with the split. Public affairs presentations in the church can symbolize the church's moral concern for the work world. Although located in a section of the country where unionism is still little understood, a small Southern church invited Victor Reuther to address one of its public forums. A St. Louis church has included symbols of the productive enterprise of the city, including the breweries, in its stained-glass windows. A church with a large percentage of its members on a university faculty organized a men's discussion lunch group on the campus—the work place, in this case.

2. There is a pastoral role related to the work world that may sometimes be played effectively through the local church. Demotion and unemployment come to the suburbanite as well as to the low-income worker in the city, although at a far less frequent rate. The moral support and the "connections" of a concerned group that gathers around the man who is discouraged can be very important. This kind of relationship can be seen in an AA group in a suburban church; alcoholism is often a related problem. In Los Angeles a voluntary association of ex-unemployed executives, Forty Plus, helps management men, suddenly out of work, find new positions. The congregation offering this kind of help must be more open on an interpersonal level than many larger suburban churches are, one in which personal failures may be honestly admitted and shared with

friends. (How sadly typical was the deacons' meeting in which an agenda item dealt with ways to make the church "more friendly," while the deacons themselves were unaware that one of their own members at the meeting was in the midst of a financial crisis in his own small business.) A large congregation fosters anonymity; we relate to parts of another person rather than to the person as a whole. However, with able pastoral leadership, the congregation ideally becomes a place in which people know one another's needs and provide encouragement that has as much significance as does help from professional employment consultants.

This is a task for laymen. In the suburb there are men with similar problems. They know about the problem of reaching the job or competence ceiling and facing it honestly, about being let off, about the business or position that is losing out in the market. The kind of pride that prevents a man from sharing these problems with another person needs steady, supportive challenging in the congregation so that when a crisis comes a man will call for help.

3. The minister of a church plays a symbolic role as well as a communications function in relating people to each other in the community of faith. Many ministers, in making it a point to know their members in their work situations, help bridge the work-suburbia separation. One minister described his second year's pattern of calling in his parish in these words (the first year's visits having been to members in their homes) :

I spoke to the president of the X company [a major employer in that community] concerning my desire to know more about the working community and lives of people working there. He arranged for me to visit the company on thirteen different Wednesdays. I visited each department of the company, meeting first with the supervisor in order to see the organization and direction of work. Then, I spent (time) with each of my parishioners. The reception was enthusiastic in every instance. This effort did much to change the life of the congregation.[30]

One Long Island pastor rides the commuter train into New York City once a week with some parishioners and spends the day in appointments of just this sort with men from the congregation.

4. The work world is recognized by the church when it utilizes the vocational skills of its members. One church-sponsored, nonprofit housing corporation in Boston, directed by blacks of the inner city, has co-opted as members of its board and as advisors in other capacities, white, middle-class suburban lawyers, contractors, and architects. A program of the Community Renewal Society of Chicago (formerly the City Mission Society) organizes several resource boards made up of suburbanites with competence in such areas as housing, job training, and education, and of an equal number of residents in the ghetto area where the program is proceeding.

5. Through identification with the whole church, Jack Browning can see himself as a part of prophetic and parabolic actions that are carried out far beyond his local congregation; some of these actions take place in relation to the work world. One significant new church frontier is found in the dozen industrial missions now established in urban centers—Boston, Detroit, Cincinnati, Philadelphia, North Carolina's Research Triangle, and others. One aspect of programming in industrial missions involves group reflection within a work level (professional, managerial, union) or within an industry across several levels (automobiles, government, electronics) designed to prompt

moral concern for the quality and meaning of life in that work-world sector. The local congregation can profit from the feedback function of any mission arm of the church, and these missions are particularly significant for the suburban church. Perspectives that are developed in the industrial mission are useful to the parish congregation, because it is there that men meet in the largest numbers with explicit religious commitments and openness to moral concerns.

Just as small groups in churches do, industrial mission groups evolve into more active roles through processes of mutual support and reflection. A recent Detroit Industrial Mission document reported such changes over the past decade. After initial research, DIM evolved from reflection in the first major stage, to a period when it served as "consultant" in industry, called on, for example, to help facilitate communications in the plant. More recently DIM has seen itself as advocate, having gained enough expertise and status to assert concern for various ways the industrial system ought to make its working operations more creative from both a human and a community point of view.[31]

A single parish minister may initiate meetings with a professional group. Hospital and university chaplains often convene such groups in two sectors of the work world— medicine and higher education. Sensitive laymen should be working out ways they themselves can prompt reflection by organizing discussion and research groups from their professional and work associates. "Sensitive" means men who are competent at their own work and who are able to help groups dig into issues of personal and social ethics.

To prompt similar initiative by its own members, a congregation should take note of worthy actions by others in the work world. Examples of creative initiative could be found in hundreds of work situations, some dramatic, others so obscure as to affect only one or two fellow workmen. Let two examples illustrate.

1. Some architects and architectural students recently walked out of a New England regional conference of the American Institute of Architects. They were attempting to raise policy questions in this professional structure and accused it of "shallow moralism and self-righteousness." "We believe," they said in a statement they released, "the architect must no longer be responsible only to the industrial and political powers, the financiers, the kings of today; nor to the professional acclaim of the magazines, but to the users, the people who inhabit the environment." [32] They were bold enough to raise broad issues of responsibility in the institutional structures of a profession. Similar debates are taking place in social work, medicine, city planning, and education.

2. At present one of the most challenging opportunities for men at several levels of industrial employment is the engrafting of new employees from the so-called "hard-core" unemployed, and the underemployed. Government funds are available for much of the cost of such attempts, but initiative from men in the management structures is essential. Exciting results are often reported alongside the inevitable disappointments. To cite but one from scores of examples, in Laurens, South Carolina, 80 of 450 responding to job-training announcements were selected. Average I.Q. was under 75 by standard testing! Seventy-two completed the ten-week course in literacy and basic education, and 68, 21 of whom had been on relief, got jobs. One estimate was that the program had created $140,000 in new yearly take-home pay. The more important dividend was the new

sense of human dignity offered to the workers. In Illinois, an executive commented on a similar program: "It's the type of thing we thought we should be involved in, even if the government hadn't joined us."

Initiatives of this sort illustrate businesslike but redemptive activity associated with the work world. One of the functions of the church is to encourage such efforts at reform. Inspired by discussions at the parish level, individuals may make changes where they work. Two of the three men whose vocational readjustments were mentioned earlier were significantly encouraged by their participation in local church study groups. The owner of a small factory testified to the help he received from a church koinonia group: "I have been able to look at my employees with different eyes. I used to want full value for full pay, but now I've seen that inefficiency may have some real causes. So I ask people into my office to find out what's the trouble. . . . Then I do what I can." [33]

In its corporate life the church celebrates God's will for integrity in human life. It articulates the final transcendence of the human spirit over the work system and every other. Here Jack Browning sings "A Mighty Fortress. . . . Let goods and kindred go." This does not free him from work or participation in the system, but it calls him to responsible, critical participation as he works. It means that his own attitude in the world will include the moods of confession and renewed commitment that are encapsulated in the cycle of worship. Such a posture, to whatever extent it is a part of a man, relates to the way he does his work, even if that worship takes place in the suburbs and no longer speaks in easy idioms like "Bringing in the Sheaves."

III | Issues in Suburban Mission

Introduction

Functionally, suburbia and central city are but two sides of a single coin named "metropolis." The jobs in business and government bureaucracies, heavy industries, and universities are mainly in the cities; and those jobs feed, clothe, and house suburban families. This unity must be recognized if the church is to help people be honest about their lives and celebrate the human community of which they are a part.

T. S. Eliot puts the moral question not just for the central city, but for the whole of the suburban-urban complex:

> When the Stranger says: "What is the meaning of this city?
> Do you huddle close together because you love each other?"
> What will you answer? "We all dwell together
> To make money from each other"? or "This is a community"? [34]

It is a false view that human life in suburbia, with all its virtues, "has it made" and can successfully cultivate peace of mind by "copping out," forgetting the city on which it so heavily depends. C. P. Snow in his 1968 address at Westminster College worried over the way the world was break-

...ng up into protectionist enclaves. "Most of us are huddling together in our own little groups for comfort's sake," he said, at a time when we should be turning outward. "We draw the curtains" creating new nationalisms and new generational antagonism.[35] Although the enclave tendency would seem anomalous because the world is shrinking rapidly, it is also the result of the shrinkage because so many pressures are brought so near. At such a time, to use a new expression emerging from our speech, "copping out" is not unnatural; it is simply immoral.

This chapter presents another set of lenses for looking at the challenge to the responsible suburban community and its church.

1. RACE

In the spring of 1968, suburban churches suddenly were challenged to confront a responsibility they had seldom openly acknowledged. The Kerner Report, a government study of the summer's violence in 1967, concluded that at root the race issue is a white problem.

> Certain fundamental matters are clear. Of these, the most fundamental is the racial attitude and behavior of white Americans toward black Americans. . . . White racism is essentially responsible for the explosive mixture which has been accumulating in our cities since the end of World War II.[36]

> Our nation is moving toward two societies, one black, one white—separate and unequal. . . . What white Americans have never fully understood—but what the Negro can never forget—is that white society is deeply implicated in the ghetto. White institutions created it, white institutions maintain it, and white society condones it.[37]

The white racism charge came at a time when the Black Power movement was making white-led social service in the black ghetto more difficult. Both the Black Power movement and the Commission report addressed white activists with the charge: "You have plenty to keep you busy healing the sick ones in your own camp. Do your thing there, and let black leaders do theirs."

Frustration mounted as white congregations reacted in two not unexpected ways. (1) "Racists?" they asked. "Us? We are not that prejudiced, and our churches have preached against discrimination for years." Or, admitting the charge (2) the churchmen asked, "How do you fight so intangible a thing as white racism?"

1. Perspective on the first reaction is important. White racism is strong language but it points to a broader problem than the blatant bigotry of a few whites. Even among enlightened whites there remains an ethnocentrism which assumes, for example, that "white" Western history is the only significant rootage of world society. The same near-sightedness fails to understand enough of the American black experience to comprehend what two psychiatrists aptly call *Black Rage*. "White racism" is perhaps inappropriately applied to the limited vision of these normal people, but with considerable justification it can be applied to the social end products. As one pastor put it, "A white racist is someone who favors civil rights but knows you have to watch out for property values."

"White racism" points to structural elements in the social system that have resulted in a lifetime of restricted opportunities for nearly every newborn black infant. Statistically, the Negro child has but half of the chance to complete high school, a third of the chance to enter one of the professions, a seventh of the chance to earn $10,000 per year as has his white counterpart.[38] He has a shorter life expectancy, more chance of being unemployed when he matures, and a far greater probability of being raised on a welfare-level income.

2. Changing unacknowledged assumptions is never easy. In fighting white racism, combating discriminatory institutional patterns is a better method than mere living room conversations about prejudice. For us to do something about today's social legacy from generations of American slavery and another century that continued to rob black people of their birthright best expresses the penitence that involvement in an immoral society must prompt in the Christian.

Prejudice and milder "racism" are matters of degree and cannot be eradicated all at once—in white or black. They involve intellect and habits of behavior in complex ways. Many "prejudiced" people can understand a particular injustice though they cannot handle rationally what to them are the overwhelming images of intermarriage and Black Power. Ask a typical small-town Southern white Christian about integration in general terms, and he will be uncomfortable; but ask him about equal pay for equal work by a black man and a white man, and he will probably come down on the side of justice. There is no need to wait for radical conversion before attacking the inequities that are clear enough to see.

The ethnic and urban history of this country has created northern cities with a characteristic pattern: a black ghetto somewhere near the center of the city surrounded by a working-class population predominantly white, and beyond that a virtually lily-white suburbia. The reasons for the pattern are historical, economic, and social. They are traceable to slavery, poverty, poor education, and untold deprivation in the rural South as well as to suburban fears and prejudices that have taken shape in the discriminatory practices of real estate agents and bankers, landlords and sellers.

This geographical shape of prejudice justifies the familiar metaphor about a white noose around the ghetto. As it is put, even by Gans, an author who does not carp at suburbia, "The suburbs have effectively zoned out the poor and the non-whites in an ever-increasing class and racial polarization of city and suburb." [39] The white population of the cities is growing much less rapidly than the national population as a whole. From 1960 to 1966 it actually declined [40] while black population in the cities increased by 20 percent. Whites are moving to the suburbs; blacks stay back.

There are, of course, an increasing number of middle-class Negroes moving to suburbia. There are both integrated churches and black churches in the suburbs. This section, however, must deal with the vastly larger number of all-white suburban congregations. The racial problem in America centers in the two-culture split between white America, epitomized in the suburbs, and the black ghetto.

There is no need to proceed to discuss at length the evils of racism in America. We must simply assume an awareness of the intensity of the crisis and the moral imperatives for programs that redress the profound grievances of this ninth of our population. Whether a person wants his language vitriolic or calm and "objective," he can find it to his liking easily enough in speeches or books by race leaders, politicians, or scholars.

Not every congregation needs to make the race issue the exclusive or even the primary aspect of its own social engagement as it cuts into human life. Iceberg-like, the issue is submerged under many others that will appear to the churchman. Treat problems of social justice—the advantaged and the disadvantaged—the race issue is there. Treat theological questions—guilt and pride and sin—and race becomes a very important illustration. It is essential, however, for every congregation to know that the race issue is urgent. That church where the very topic of race is taboo is too closed and insecure to serve redemptively either its own members or its community.

The white congregation that deals explicitly with the race issue will be helped by acknowledging the mix of personal and public elements in the "white racism" of its members. We may illustrate this mix with some reflections on the nature of white suburbia.

1. Suburbs are the native habitat of strong privatist emotions. Homes take on the aspect of nests and retreats and castles—places isolated from the conflicts of the public world in which the turbulent evolution toward racial justice is so important. This feeling for home is extended to the neighborhood. Thus whites can see the arrival of but a single black family into "our" block as an intrusion from the public world. They will fight and protest the sale of a house to a Negro family when there would be no equally possessive presumption to judge whether or not that house should be sold to any other white family.[41]

It is in the intimacy of the private world that the psychological roots of prejudice run deepest. "Would you want your daughter to marry a Negro?" Ultimately, until intermarriage is thoroughly embraced in principle and is more common in practice, stereotypical division of people on the basis of color and resulting racist behavior will be a significant factor in American public life. Racism will be with us until anxious parents no longer plant the seeds of prejudice in their children. Ten-year-old Johnny talks in play-world fantasy about Susan, a black classmate; but even a "liberal" parent says, "Johnny, Susan has fine parents and is a lovely girl, but Negroes and white people don't get married when they grow up." And Johnny begins to think in terms of color.

Currently, the movement toward black self-consciousness makes for black disavowal of exogamy. Such a move is necessary to combat the self-denigration, conscious or unconscious, bred in many black children by the culture. "Black is beautiful." "Racist" though this black-consciousness is, it is a means for counteracting the effects of a color-conscious, racist society. We cannot ultimately be content, however, until a healthy pluralism leads to easier personal acceptance between self-respecting individuals in an open society, and intermarriage seems no more questionable than the marriages of redheads to brunettes.[42] Christian ethics affirms that there is neither Greek nor Jew nor black nor white.

Color blindness comes slowly on intimate interpersonal levels. White suburbia contributes to structural racism because of its privatist propensities.

2. Suburbia is often newly established and heavily mortgaged. Property values therefore are a special source of anxiety for the suburbanite, especially the mobile resident who buys and sells his house like an automobile. The myth about property values in integrated neighborhoods is fed with the fears of losing money in the next transaction.

Research studies explode this myth as fantasy born of anxiety and prejudice. By comparison with control neighborhoods, which have no influx of black homeowners, property values generally keep pace or rise more rapidly in neighborhoods into which Negroes have moved.[43]

Again, an activist approach to this issue is best. The presence of a Negro family in a neighborhood is a better antidote to prejudice than a hundred sermons. Those agencies which help black families move to white suburban areas not only achieve fair treatment for their clients but they do a significant educational service as well. Church backing for these agencies attacks racism.

3. Because prejudice is a matter of attitude, one misleading statement has it that "you can't change a man's heart by law." Basic attitudes are not usually affected directly by law, although the educative effect of the law is not to be discounted; but attitudes are modified by experience, and law so affects the social order as to modify human experience. When modification of law or institutional policy effects integration without waiting for all the "hearts" involved to change, attitudes change as a result of changed experience. The public's changing assumptions about the racial makeup of "normal" apartment houses, classrooms, and work groups result from new situations created by new law. Man is a psychosocial creature, and the traffic between the domain of "heart" and "law" flows both ways.

At present, most men and women of the black ghetto are hardly concerned about whether or not white hearts are changed. Justice is their concern, and there is no question but that legal remedies are often wholly appropriate. When a registrar in the South makes it more difficult for blacks to vote than for whites, or when a licensed realtor in the North does injury to blacks by denying them service, justice is thwarted. Law is properly invoked.

Furthermore, law reinforces personal attitude in important ways. The unheroic realtor who wants to sell without discriminating may be right when he insists that he will lose more business than he can afford if he obeys only his conscience. A law may tip the balance by giving him one more reason to justify moral action: "I had to do it; it's the law."

4. A further illustration of the public and private mix of racism is found in suburban education. The child in all-white suburbia picks up a distorted image of his culture. He tends to think of America as a white nation. Until recently he was likely to find that distorted picture in his textbooks themselves. Even with multiethnic study materials, however, lack of experience with a multiracial group subtly provides for the child a false image of "normal" American population groups. Black people are strangers to him.

A four-year study of intergroup experience and learning by school children of a representative suburban community reports:

> The average elementary-school child in New Village does not know and has never known a Negro his own age. . . . Racial ignorance and racial prejudice flourished among the young children there. . . . Children at the very earliest age had learned to look upon Negroes as different, inferior, undesirable and even violent. . . . This . . . mirrors the attitudes of the adult community. . . . Parents . . . paid lip service to ideas of racial justice, but admitted to prejudice on closer questioning.[44]

Similar problems present themselves in regard to limited preparation for pluralistic ethnic and religious society. As for economic differences, "The children of New Village knew almost nothing about persons less well off than themselves." Shown pictures of sharecroppers' children, one class concluded that they had to be foreigners. No American children would be so poor.[45]

In the light of the inadequacy of classroom and community experience as a preparation for life in a multiracial nation, the summary of this Columbia University study was well titled: "The Short-changed Children of Suburbia." The U.S. Commission on Civil Rights reached a similar conclusion after its study on *de facto* segregation in schools across the country:

> There is evidence in this report which suggests that children educated in all-white institutions are more likely than others to develop racial fears and prejudices based upon lack of contact and information. Although it cannot be documented in traditional ways, we believe that white children are deprived of something of value when they grow up in isolation from children of other races, when their self-esteem and assurance may rest in part upon false notions of racial superiority, when they are not prepared by their school experience to participate fully in a world rich in human diversity. These losses, although not as tangible as those which racial isolation inflicts upon Negro youngsters, are real enough to deserve the attention of parents concerned about their children's development.[46]

Current suburban-urban programs of cooperation in educational parks and the bussing of inner-city children to suburban schools will not solve the massive problems of urban education. They are, however, significant steps to counteract unconscious racism in some children. Church action has fostered such steps in several parts of the country.

What will the leadership in a responsible white suburban congregation do in relation to this "American Dilemma"— that society and church are segregated in spite of creeds demanding an open and reconciled society?

1. To begin at the most modest level, the race issue will be on the agenda. Preaching and teaching, and fellowship groups will deal with it. The congregation at large may be conservative and relatively uninvolved, but even to read

announcements of discussions helps prevent the head-in-sand assumption that a Christian congregation can go its way while skirting such a major concern in the life of the society around it. A church newsletter presents to its readers something of an image of what "church" is all about. It may therefore be expected to have in it a healthy balance of newsworthy concern for parishioners one by one (the sick, the bereaved) and the common life (racial justice, public welfare, war and peace) alongside more routine matters of a Christian congregation (baptisms, marriages, the liturgical year).

News items and talk alone, however, are not the best way to become acquainted with a crucial issue of public life. *De facto* segregation is so thoroughgoing in our society that it can be assumed in most white congregations that most members do not know any black people personally. Hence contact itself is a legitimate concern in programming.

Black leaders are properly sensitive to the ways some Negroes have been "used" by white congregations. From the white side, however, it is fair to argue the importance of some personal contact with blacks on an equal footing if personal racist attitudes are finally to be fought on every level. One white college student from the South had been formally taught in both school and church the standard creeds of democracy and brotherhood. Yet he demonstrated after a single 45-minute period in an integrated church group the immense learning that takes place in experience. Tragic as are the implications of his comment, there is life-changing liberation reflected in it too: "I always was afraid someday I would have to sit next to a colored guy; but you know, there's nothing to it."

What is easily possible to the typical suburban church is

the intentional inclusion of black speakers, resource people, and guests in study groups, in the pulpit, and in forums presented for the community. Leaders responsible for youth conferences or area meetings of laymen will have a special concern that Negro churchmen be present in the group. Joint meetings of youth groups, exchanging choirs, cooperative vacation programs—while none of these directly tackles the most crucial concerns of the moment, nonetheless they provide means for the erosion of suburban racism.

2. White America's "awareness gap" should lead churches into programs emphasizing the black heritage in our national life. Church groups may help initiate high school elective courses or community groups for the study of black history.

One white suburban church sponsored a "black heritage day" built around a division of Negro history into five epochs. After presentations of African dances by a black group from the city, and a very brief statement about the course of black history, participants were assigned to five different groups. Each "class" went to a room in which there were pictures and music from a particular period in black history. After a fifteen-minute presentation by well-prepared leaders, black and white, everyone present was given paper and paint and invited to interpret with his drawing or painting the feeling or the ideas he had developed about that particular part of the black struggle. Finally, before a fellowship meal, the contributions were all posted in appropriate groupings in the main hall of the church. Enough black youths and adults were involved as leaders and guests that the whole program was integrated as well as lively, timely, and highly communicative.

Every suburban church library should consider subscribing to some of the periodicals of the black press such as

Ebony and *Crisis* and local newspapers from the black sector of the metropolitan community. Study groups can use significant paperbacks, novels and nonfiction alike: James Baldwin's *Go Tell It on the Mountain,* Claude Brown's *Manchild in the Promised Land,* Martin Luther King's *Why We Can't Wait,* Ralph Ellison's *The Invisible Man,* John Griffin's *Black Like Me,* Malcolm X's *Autobiography,* C. Eric Lincoln's *The Black Muslims in America,* C. Vann Woodward's *The Strange Career of Jim Crow.* Other scholarly but readable documents should be considered by even the small church library—Gunnar Myrdal's *An American Dilemma,* W. E. Du Bois' *Souls of Black Folk,* Kenneth Clark's *Dark Ghetto,* and the newer works that present black history and the Negro heritage for juveniles and adults.

3. Most activists concerned for the race issue will probably work through ad hoc human relations groups in the suburb or the metropolis, but it is valuable for congregational units to be involved as well. Action on social structures is more difficult for most churches than the internal educational programs described above, and it may require groupings that have an autonomous status outside congregational control. Normally, however, a social action committee within a church should have the freedom to sponsor studies and move to action in its own name without waiting for concensus in the whole congregation. For example, a committee might launch research on the bussing of inner-city children to suburban schools, and then either sponsor a broader community study or issue a report to the congregation and community on its findings with a proposal for action.

A social action group within a church should find ways to challenge the congregation at large with opportunities for more direct involvement in the racial issue. If there is church money in invested funds, the committee may propose that some of it be invested in explicitly integrationist enterprises. M–Reit (Mutual Real Estate Investment Trust) is one such firm, a successful national corporation specializing in operating middle-class apartment buildings on an integrated basis and steadily seeking funds to expand into unintegrated white urban areas. A Peabody, Massachusetts, Jewish temple purchased a block of shares in a newly formed biracial bank in a ghetto area of Boston. Church funds may be invested closer home in nonprofit and limited-dividend housing corporations in the central city; if properly interpreted, the involvement will represent not only better housing for low-income black people but a meaningful step for the congregation.

Families in the suburban congregation can volunteer to receive Friendly Town children from the inner city for a week's "vacation" in the summer. (Friendly Town programs usually bring black ghetto children to live with suburban or small-town families.) After their experience, the families should report to the congregation at large and invite others to participate. Some suburban churches have organized entire camping experiences for their own and inner-city children together. Those Friendly Town programs do more than provide new experiences for children. They help bridge the communication gap between ghetto and suburb. One affluent father discovered that his ghetto counterpart in Chicago was paying exorbitant rent for a run-down house; he proceeded to purchase the structure, rehabilitate it, and reduce the rent.

Many congregations have taken a significant step by participating in Project Equality, a program in several regions of the country. Denominations and local churches agree that in all their buying and contracting they will limit themselves to equal-opportunity firms, firms approved as such by regional Project Equality offices. The Methodist Conference of Baltimore (720 churches) recently approved a stringent resolution limiting all future construction to contractors with fair-employment practices, the building contracts to include equalized "employment, upgrading, recruiting, apprenticeship" and other provisions. The temporal power of most congregations is not large, but what there is can be used for justice.

Operation Breadbasket, launched by the Southern Christian Leadership Conference before the death of Martin Luther King, Jr., is forming small business investment corporations among blacks to utilize help from governmental and private sources in building greater black economic strength. Jesse Jackson, one of the Breadbasket leaders, urges white churches to take the initiative and join with black churches in establishing banks. He wrote in 1968 that altogether the twenty-six Negro banks in America did not have the assets of one major bank in the city of Chicago.[47] The social action committee of a church may want to remind the congregation at a time when new personnel is sought, whether on the professional, clerical, or janitorial level, that it must not be unconsciously limited to white people in its search. The committee may propose an intentional search for a black employee.

4. On a yet more substantial level, direct relationships with the inner city may be studied and developed by the congregation. The ghetto is the key to catching up for the American Negro; most of the next generations will grow up there, even if the number "escaping" to integrated and middle-class America should multiply many times.

These relationships take careful *cooperative* planning between suburban leaders and others who are from the ghetto. One suburban church in South Glastonbury, Connecticut, found resistance to the Project Equality proposal in argument that it was too little a step, and too petty. In the standoff, it was proposed that something more significant be done and a salary be raised to put a man at the disposal of a church in the Hartford ghetto. The proposal was adopted. This staff man has facilitated highly significant suburban-urban cooperation. Volunteers from South Glastonbury and elsewhere serve alongside ghetto residents in activities that this minister makes possible.

It must be emphasized that currents of learning and respect must flow both ways in such suburban-urban relationships. One ghetto leader training volunteers from the suburbs said, "We won't put these people to work in the city until they realize they are a part of the problem and have a lot to learn." "When they work in our program," said another, "suburbanites come up against a looser style leadership than they are used to and they learn to face unexpected crises without panicking because their schedule is disrupted. They learn patience and insight into less obvious successes, like simple ability to control oneself and cope with life in face of the frustrations in the ghetto. They learn new respect for the magnificent people who live here."

I asked a black parent in one inner-city neighborhood about current fears that whites could be of no help because of increasing black consciousness. "No," she said, "that's not true. We need help with the problems we face, and when we work together, the whites are O.K. They don't always understand how it is in this neighborhood, but they sometimes know helpful people and know some ways to do things that are important for us to learn." Another leader,

a militant black pastor, emphasized that race is not the
problem but person-to-person openness. When a white student said he found himself ineffective in a ghetto youth can-
teen, the minister said: "It's not your color; it's something
else. I know whites who do it. As the kids say, 'They're not
white.' "

The suburban church is on the front line in the battle
against white racism. It is a major community institution
where public opinion is expressed and affected. Public
opinion is not a chance thing, as all advertisers and public
relations men are aware. The church, destroyed if it sur-
vives or grows by a public-relations adjustment to the mind-
set of the world around it, is yet charged with persuading
men toward the mind-set "that was in Christ." It is therefore in the communications business—like it or not. If responsible, it will consciously review the impact of its life
and program upon the world around. It must ask whether
by action or inaction it helps sustain a separatist and racially oppressive life in the society or asserts, for its own
community to hear and feel, a challenge to our racism. "If
we are not part of the answer, we are part of the problem."

Race is a major concern of the church for more reasons
than the economic and social injustice it foments in our
society. The way American suburbanites relate to the race
issue can toughen and deepen their religious perspective in
three important ways.

Guilt and repentance. One urban missioner, in arguing
the plausibility of a particular program among whites, said,
"There is still a lot of guilt we can capitalize on." He was
right of course, but his comment prompts reflection on the
motivation of white suburbanites who act on the racial
front. There is a difference between guilt feelings and penitence; the latter is a posture of humility and renewal that

accepts the burden of change. "I rejoice," Paul wrote the Corinthians, "not because you were grieved, but because you were grieved into repenting; for you felt a Godly grief. . . . Godly grief produces a repentance that leads to salvation and brings no regret, but worldly grief produces death." (II Cor. 7:9-10.)

Projects for the expiation of guilt are likely to be short-lived; the fruits of repentance last longer. Such an interpretation of racism as will lead to repentance is the particular vocation of the church.

The missioner is justified in his comment because even short-lived guilt may lead to some support for worthwhile efforts in the ghetto—like a day-long clean-up, fix-up effort by several thousand New York suburbanites who came into town after Martin Luther King's assassination. The danger is that the impulse behind the help will not move on into structural changes and that once spent it will make for self-righteousness if the little projects "don't do any good."

If the black experience is taken to heart by America, we as a nation may see in this long and tragic struggle toward freedom the "true epic poem of our American history" [48] and thereby gain a new vision of our anguished hope for greatness. Whites have the choice of identifying with the prodigal son or with the elder brother; only the first will do.

Power. We perennially confuse love with sentimentality. We overlook the necessity for justice within love. In the name of "love" the white Southerner has insisted on face-to-face pleasantries from the black when anger was necessary if honesty and the black man's self-respect were to be preserved. In the name of "love" the Northerner has resisted use of law to open doorways to equality, thinking that love meant persuasion alone. "Too much love," quoted one black leader, "Too much love/Nothing kills a Nigger/Like too much love." [49]

We need a tough understanding of love in suburban America, one tempered with an understanding of that Jesus who taught about rich men, camels, and the needle's eye, the first being last and the last first. From the Black Power movement white Christians should relearn the relation of love to justice, seeing in properly used earthly power echoes of a power that works for righteousness and therefore for man's wholeness.

Understanding the sentimental corruption of love will help the church recover from its evasion of politics. Assisting the underrepresented and the powerless is a political affair. The church that avoids politics because of a sentimentalized understanding of love leaves its institutionalized strength on the side of the *status quo*. It makes a political choice by default and resigns from its critical, prophetic vocation.

Facing up to the reality of structural racism is a means for the church to move beyond not only the privatism of the suburban ethos but privatism in its theology. Such privatism characterizes Protestant individualism which thinks of worship as nothing but a gathering of people engaged in personal devotions. It fails to see an institutional role for the church in the culture well beyond the "inspiration" of its members to sober living, good citizenship, and personal good works. We need a more political theology.

Style. Assimilation into the dominant white culture has been the destiny of most immigrant groups, but the native-born Negro group finds this avenue closed. In the immediate future at least, a different kind of adjustment, that of pluralism, is the Negro goal.[50] A positive gain for our life-style can result. Just as "copping out" emerges meaningfully from common speech, so does another vernacular expression: "soul." Soul can be seen as an alternative to an up-tight stereotype: white, Anglo-Saxon, Protestant. In this usage, soul transcends its racial connotations and softens the undesirable elements in WASPish American culture.

Preston Williams, of Boston University, has suggested [51] that soul implies (1) a desire for intimate friendships rather than formal ones, (2) the appreciation of natural pleasures rather than artificial ones, and (3) the spontaneous, the emotional, and the expressive, as compared to the repressive, the ordered, and the "reasonable." If so, soul answers more than black needs. As it has in music already, soul may contribute redemptively to the cultural style.

White America desperately needs black America. As James Baldwin described it eloquently a decade ago:

> What it comes to is that if we, who can scarcely be considered a white nation, persist in thinking of ourselves as one, we condemn ourselves, with the truly white nations . . . to sterility and decay, whereas if we could accept ourselves *as we are,* we might bring new life to the Western achievements and transform them. The price of this transformation is the unconditional freedom of the Negro; it is not too much to say that he, who has been so long rejected, must now be embraced, and at no matter what psychic or social risk. He is *the* key figure in his country, and the American future is precisely as bright or as dark as his.[52]

A suburban congregation through its involvement with the race issue can gain a new appreciation of repentance, a new understanding of love and power, and a richer life-style to complement what has been called the bureaucratic personality of our time. Ultimately that kind of change will serve some of the deepest spiritual needs in the white population. It will move us beyond the blindness and anxiety

by virtue of which we have contributed, sometimes unaware, to the personal and structural racism that afflicts our
land.

2. HOUSING

A two-way relation binds housing to life-style. Housing
expresses the values of the people who build and buy it. On
the other hand, a neighborhood of houses affects the lives
of people who live there. For these reasons there is a morality to housing patterns in suburbia. The suburban community—through its planners and developers, zoning commission members, social activists, and others—needs to step
back the way an anthropologist does, looking at its own
"human settlement" and asking questions: What does our
housing say about the values we hold? How does it affect us?

The suburbanite invests enormous concern in his housing. One classic study asserted that for the upper-range
suburbanites in *Crestwood Heights* the possession of the
house is what makes psychologically possible the "Crestwood way of life." The authors emphasize the expressive
nature of the housing. "We may compare the house . . .
to a stage and the people present to characters who are dis-
playing the parts they play in the community at large." The
Crestwood house is not a place where these adults grew
up. It has no old-shoe feel to it. It is an "apparatus" fur-
nished and designed by the new owners.

Most suburbanites are not in the Crestwood Heights
class and most community analysts are not as psychologically oriented as the authors of that study. Herbert Gans,
writing about Levittowners, spends very little time on the
house as such. But the *House Beautiful* style of magazine

and general American standards (wall-to-wall carpeting, stereo-TV consoles, family rooms, patios) demonstrate that a major suburbanite preoccupation is in the housing he is able to provide for himself. William Dobriner stresses the visual openness of suburbia, and, like Whyte, its effect on social grouping and the sense of community.

An attempt at moral reflection on suburban housing must go beyond commentary on the emotional and financial investment it represents and beyond sociological recognition of the effects that visual openness and friendship patterns have on people in suburbia. Housing and the temptations to enclave living are intimately related. No one has described the feeling for home that is a part of the suburban mood better than has Gibson Winter. Winter argues that urban life depends upon a web of impersonal relationships, such as contacts between store clerks and customers, between government people and the public, and among fellow passengers on the subway. But people

> need to be more than the impersonal function they perform. They need to be evaluated for *who they are* as well as *what they can do*. They have to *be* as well as *do*. These deep needs for stability, recognition, and familiarity in personal associations lead to desires for continuing neighborhood relationships; in fact, they lead to a struggle for homogeneous neighborhoods.[53]

When they perceive variety in the neighborhood as a threat to their own self-esteem, people can make of it an enclave that ruptures broader human community. The struggle for these homogeneous and stable neighborhoods, says Winter, "has made segregation along racial and/or class lines endemic to the metropolis." Another writer calls the suburbs "monuments to white anxiety."

The extent to which this kind of motivation is behind the

suburban migration is debatable. The suburban myth spoke of a "flight" to the suburbs in judgmental terms, and it saw deep currents of nostalgia for small-town community in the retreat as well. Gans argues, however, that the New Jersey Levittowners "wanted a new house, but not a new life, and the community they established was not particularly novel." [54] Their move was not a flight from city life, but a plain quest for better housing. The homogeneity provided by suburbia did foster more "neighboring" and friendships. "We see eye to eye on things, about raising kids, doing things together with your husband, living the same way; we have practically the same identical background." [55] However, these people were not looking for an idyllic setting or a consumption-centered life, or "roots" and a "sense of community." "Mainly they came for a house and not a social environment," Gans summarizes, and he notes a similar conclusion from Crestwood Heights.[56]

Winter is right, nonetheless, that "home" means something of a retreat from the outside world. Home is a place of intimacy where the adult or the child finds acceptance that allows him to discard some of the defenses and the striving of the public world. The family unit functions to restore confidence, to bathe wounds; it offers shoulders to cry on, laps to sit on, the enveloping arms of affection. It maintains and nourishes life for risky goal-seeking activity in the outside world and for adjustment to the pressures of that world. It is a womb of protection and sleep.

Projections of these feelings about home onto the neighborhood account for the way suburbia tends to become an enclave. It is good, not bad, that homes renew us for life in the wider world. This is an active function, however. The womb is a generative, muscular organ, not a mere receptacle, and the love that we find in a home and a neighborhood ought to be muscular and structured rather than merely sentimental. This means we favor an open neighborhood rather than an enclave. The Christian knows that sentimental love is demonic if it draws rigid circles labeled "enemy" and "friend." Jesus' ethic in the Sermon on the Mount denies that limited "love" of one's own kind is love, for God "sends rain on the just and on the unjust," and that is a model for love.

Protective and exclusive neighborhoods reinforce in both children and adults the closure of false love that is opposed to the "far" neighbors beyond the lines of the nearest class or creedal or ethnic group. Limited experience is one of the elements of deprivation for the "short-changed children of suburbia," secure and loving as the homes and classrooms may be.

The ethics of racial exclusion from suburban neighborhoods needs little elaboration at this point. The Supreme Court ruled out legal enforcement of racially restrictive deeds in 1949. There are progressive elements in the National Association of Real Estate Boards that are now aware of the need to counteract the racial and religious exclusion once enunciated in the professional ethic and even echoed into the 1940's in federal mortgage insurance regulations.[57]

"Open housing," of course, is no settled matter in the public mind. California's passionate struggle over Proposition 14 illustrates not only the power of a conservative real estate industry but the fear and moral bankruptcy of large numbers of white people on so clear-cut an issue as that of a housing market open to all. Rationalizations about individual property rights, when they yield structural racism in housing, misunderstand the function of democratic government. Democratic law must maintain the just rights of the minority; without this, a nation moves toward fascistic tyranny by the majority. Racial integration of the suburbs is slow in coming for many reasons, but there is no question about the moral necessity for open housing. "Is your neighborhood white or all-American?"

A more difficult issue is that of exclusion on the basis of economic class. Around the American city today there is a middle- and an upper-class noose as well as a white one. This is primarily the result of the inability of low-income groups to afford basic middle-class housing, but zoning practices in many suburbs go to intolerable extremes. Some upper-class suburbs are so notoriously restrictive that the public school ethos matches that of exclusive private schools. Only the very well-to-do can contemplate buying into these communities.

The more numerous main-line suburbs of the middle class also offer no access for the poor. "What else would you have us do?" is a natural question of the conscientious planning commission member in such a community. "Housing is a part of a good environment; we know the injustice and disruption that result from mixed usage, from the absence of strict housing codes and the failure to establish neighborhood uniformities in building standards and lot sizes." We confront here another pattern in which apparently conscientious policy produces structural injustice.

Street by street, this planning commission member is more or less right. However, the power of the state is immorally used if it exploits one group of people in the society. Legal boundaries like those of a suburb may be misused this way. Urban residents are discriminated against if middle-class suburbs universally force lower-income groups to remain within the city while they siphon off the leadership and financial resources of the middle and upper classes. One of the major issues in legislative and judicial process will soon be found to center on this question of the rights of an incorporated suburb to zone out normal elements of the total community. A court has already told one suburb that it cannot zone out a college population from its midst. State legislatures are receiving proposals designed to prevent towns from totally excluding certain types of housing that would facilitate a more balanced population mix. In 1966 the Conference of City Mayors asked the Federal Government to withhold grants to suburban towns unless they agreed to provide a "reasonable share" of low-income housing in their area.[58] In Connecticut, it was proposed recently that the zoning power of municipalities be subject to the condition that "in every municipality the construction of multiple-family dwelling units shall be permitted on at least 10 percent of all land zoned for residential use."

Gans, reflecting upon housing patterns in places like Levittown, agrees that people are happier in a neighborhood of homes of similar size and cost. He found, however, that the "neighborhood" in this case can be a very small unit, only a city block or two in size. The next homes may be of a higher- or lower-income level with little difficulty. There is no need for a high-income level in the entire community.

Yet another moral dimension of the suburban-housing picture has to do with popular attitudes toward government policy. Suburbia has attracted new residents because of cheaper land, more space, usually lower taxes. It has also been the recipient of direct subsidies in the form of federal mortgage insurance for its housing and indirect assistance through highway construction that has enhanced both suburban access to the city and suburban land values. In 1957, of about 107 billion dollars in mortgage debt, over 47 billion dollars was in FHA-insured and VA-guaranteed loans that favored single-family homes. That meant subsidy for moving to suburbia, because land has not been widely available in the cities. It is important for suburbanites to recognize this when they encounter reactionary opinion criticizing subsidies for the city resident. Subsidies for suburbanites have been subsidies not available to the poor. Senator Ribicoff estimated in the late '60s that it took an annual income of about $8,000 to *qualify* for the then current federal "subsidies" for housing mortgages, an income level that excluded over half—the poorer half—of the American people.[59]

Churches have probably been more deeply involved in housing than in any other aspect of the contemporary urban crisis. The structure of federal housing assistance has required local initiative by nonprofit groups. The staff and voluntaristic energies available through congregations and denominations have met the need well. Churches have been stronger and quicker to move on the housing front than civic clubs, trade unions, human relations councils, and the like. One housing expert estimates that 75 percent of the nonprofit housing corporations across the country were formed on church initiative.

Both the frustrations of activists in the civil rights struggle and the evolving climate of ecumenism have fostered action in housing. Better housing has been a concrete step of social amelioration for income groups below the mean, one that usually sidestepped direct confrontation with white opposition to racial integration in white neighborhoods.

A few illustrative patterns will demonstrate the range of possibilities for church involvement in housing. In Pittsburgh, churches and organizations from all three faith groups sponsor or project the construction of over 900 housing units for low-income and moderate-income families. Included in the figure are rent-supplement apartments for families with incomes under $5,000 a year, a 156-unit residence for the elderly handicapped initiated by the Order of Franciscan Nuns, 160 rehabilitated homes, and new construction of several hundred units in renewal areas. Some former Protestant church sites are being donated to the Housing Authority to use for low-income developments.

In the city-suburb of Oakland, California, there is underway a fully staffed senior center with 150 apartments. Sixty-two outlying churches that are part of the Satellite Senior Homes help arrange activities and services for residents of nearby smaller satellite projects, nine of which are finally to be built. Oakland has 91,000 older people, half of whom in 1968 had an annual income of less than $1,000 per person.

In Springfield, Massachusetts, and in Baltimore, nonprofit groups are helping responsible low-income families work toward home ownership. Springfield's Micah, named for the Old Testament prophet, encourages work in rehabilitation of housing by the tenant himself and credits this labor in dollar terms as "sweat equity" toward the down payment. By the beginning of 1969 twenty-three low-income families had been enabled to make the move to home ownership, and forty-six more had leased with purchase options that they expected to exercise within about a year, all this without public subsidy.

Motivation to assist people toward home ownership is high among most suburbanites, themselves homeowners. Moreover, home ownership is a key to maintaining or upgrading the lower-income areas of the city. "The prime generator of good maintenance is owner-residence," one study of slum housing in Newark concluded. "It is only this factor that produces the degree of close supervision required for good maintenance of slum properties." [60]

HOPE, in Baltimore, announces its purposes in this concise statement:

> Home Ownership Plan Endeavor, Inc., [HOPE], is a non-profit organization designed to make decent, low-cost homes available to deserving low-income families in the Baltimore metropolitan area. . . . Working through social agencies, churches, and other referral groups, HOPE selects families whose need for decent housing is clear, and whose ability to maintain reasonable payments is demonstrable. Each of these families is offered an appropriate house at a rate which it can pay. (In each case, this rate is based on HOPE's expenditure to acquire the mortgage on the house and to make essential repairs.) In simplest terms, HOPE enables families who have no down payment to occupy at once good homes they can eventually own.

Both groups are financed through low-income debentures sold to the general public. Churches and church-individuals are the heaviest purchasers.

The most important part of all the widespread activity these citations represent is the decent housing provided to persons otherwise poorly housed and often financially exploited. One 13-member family HOPE helped had paid $15 a week for a dismal cramped four-room apartment until HOPE arranged for a 10-room house in excellent condition at $17 a week.

By-products are also significant, however. One more sector of the economy, once considered exclusively a sphere for profit-taking free enterprise, is being subordinated to the more rational processes that have human welfare as the goal. The low-income end of the housing market is being somewhat removed from the price system and opened up to assistance from dedicated individuals and nonprofit organizations and from the public at large through governmental transfer payments (tax money that subsidizes low-interest mortgages). There is no need for low-income families to be deprived of decent housing in a society as well-off as ours.

Involving churches in the process of using humane criteria to modify a purely free market system in housing can provide significant educative experience for many ideologically conservative churchmen. Seeing what can be done by government and nonprofit groups in cooperation with each other will help prepare the typical suburbanite to understand housing as something of a public service or a regulated utility in the case of families too poor to manage in the open market where limited urban space creates the conditions for rent gouging. Through medicare we have removed human health from the vagaries of our price system; housing for the poor is next in line.

There is enormous need for larger housing effort in this country. One church-sponsored nonprofit report, for example, reads as follows:

> The South End is an urban renewal area in which 3500 households will be displaced by renewal activity over the next seven years. . . . About ⅔ or 2300 of these displaced households will have incomes which make them eligible for public housing. Yet there are only 800 units of new public housing to be built in the area.[61]

The story could be duplicated in city after city on a larger or a smaller scale. Church involvement in these problems will help lead to national concern and larger appropriations to meet the need.

Yet another benefit from suburban church involvement in housing is the satisfaction people derive from their efforts. Many a businessman or professional feels himself trapped in a large corporation with built-in goals of profit-seeking as the primary test of success. If he participates in a nonprofit venture like Micah, he can use business skills in his leisure time for more creative ends.

The least threatening housing proposals for suburban sponsorship are those involving assistance to the elderly. There is a tradition for communal religious assistance to the aged through "church homes." Area-wide action through church judicatories or ecumenical organization is easily feasible on these popular projects. Such regional co-operation in itself helps counteract suburban isolation. If the units are in suburbia, they may help the suburb welcome new low-income immigrants from the city.

Once launched on an interest in housing, most groups will begin learning that the needs are larger and different than they had at first imagined. In one Eastern suburb, the second ring out from the city, a group began with a modest concern for a few old people, most of whom had moved out from the first-ring suburbs where living costs had risen too high for them. "It was a revelation to us to discover how many limited-income people we have in our town," said one committee member who had helped on the project. "We will have rent-supplement people living in our development. The widows find that the pensions stop when their husbands die, and the social security goes down. They can't live where they did before. Another thing—this project has brought both ends of town together. Few things do that around here."

Recent housing legislation at the federal level has begun to overleap city boundaries in its assistance to low-income groups as earlier laws did not. Formerly, housing aid to the poor was available through housing authorities with jurisdiction only in the city that set them up. The poor had to stay in the city. These housing authorities can still assist a family with rent supplements by contracting for a rental unit beyond the city limits only if that neighboring town officially sanctions such an arrangement. This constitutes a challenge to suburban action groups. Housing supplements are primarily a federal welfare program. Therefore it is an artificial restriction if a family is not free to cross a city line when desirable housing that otherwise qualifies for rent-supplement programs is available.[62]

Our long-range task in housing the poor involves research and planning and politicking. If the cities are not to be overwhelmingly burdened with the poor, and if the poor are not to be altogether deprived of the advantages inherent in middle-class communities, the present barriers to more housing for low-income groups in the suburbs must be further lowered.[63]

As a suburb grows we must ask whether it is possible for a cross section of the society to find housing within its borders. This means a conscious effort to supplement the more luxurious residential market with housing that is within reach of the lower middle-class groups as well as legislation encouraging nonprofit groups to house low- and low-moderate-income families within the suburb.

The new towns of Reston, Virginia, and Columbia, Maryland, will not be full cross sections of the American class system by any means, but they avoid the worst features of the exclusive suburbs from which even the local public school teachers are sometimes economically excluded. Row houses and apartments are built alongside the more typical one-family detached housing. In Reston, two federally subsidized apartment developments were projected for 1970, one (198 units) for families with incomes from $6200 to $11,500, the other (235 units) for households in which at least one member of the family must be sixty-two years old or older and in which the income is not over $4800. The conditions of the contract between Reston developers and the U.S. Geological Survey, which is locating 2500 employees in the town, requires more low- and moderate-income housing in the near future.

Whereas some developers argue that in a given new neighborhood house prices should not vary more than $3,000 to $5,000, in Reston homes in the mid-twenties range are set side by side with others that sell for well over $40,000. A participant in the Reston development team reports hearing no comments from buyers or prospective buyers criticizing this kind of price range.[64]

In Columbia, now in its early stages but destined to become a city of 110,000, the nonprofit Columbia Interfaith Housing Corporation has already sponsored 300 low-rent town house units in the first of nine "villages" that will eventually make up the city. The Columbia Cooperative Ministry, in which thirteen denominational bodies are pooling their resources for religious witness and community service, hopes to help assure in Columbia a pluralistic society in which a wide range of people can find acceptance and dignity.

The responsible suburban church will have no unique wisdom to offer planners and developers and legislators as they make decisions affecting the human settlements of metropolis. It will, however, highlight the moral issues in housing and it can often serve itself as a voluntary nonprofit sponsor for significant housing ventures on behalf of the under classes in our affluent society.

3. Localism, Metropolis, and a Serious Call

Should I enlarge my own suburban home while people in the city live in substandard housing? when many in the world are homeless? Should we with tax revenue enrich our suburban schools for ourselves when urban schools desperately need more money? How much political power is best kept here, how much better shared with metropolis?

The Christian posture. Localism fits within the Christian dilemma of the near neighbor and the far one. Self-deceiving pretensions at righteousness fall to either side in this dilemma. A man may be so involved in social causes on behalf of distant neighbors that he neglects his own family and violates commitments he has assumed in marriage and parenthood. More often the error is to the other side; we give our all for the family—clothing and sport cars and summer camps and a larger house every fifth year—while a relatively near neighbor wants for a pair of shoes.

Christians discover that Jesus puts this near-neighbor–far-neighbor problem under perennial scrutiny. The true neighbor is the traveler on the road to Jericho who has compassion on a man beyond the circle of his fellow priests, fellow Levites, and fellow countrymen. The gospel's injunction is explicitly to show love for that man who is so far from us that we designate him nonneighbor—an "enemy." God sends on him also the rain and the sun, making him our neighbor.

How to love justly both the far neighbor and the near one becomes the substance of our ethical reasoning once the stance of love is affirmed. This posture of love means that we have rejected the hedonistic alternatives that disclaim neighbor love as an obligation. It means, on the other hand, that without despair or cynicism we acknowledge our inability fully to live up to that norm. Otherwise, this moral commitment becomes unbearably oppressive rather than liberating. Dare I buy a single business suit when one starving distant neighbor sleeps hungry in a Calcutta gutter? Grace means that we are freed from a constant nagging of self-doubt and anxiety, a "wallowing in concern about the appropriateness of our decisions," as one theologian put it. Karl Barth called the command of God a "festive invitation"; it is not an oppressive law.

The nearest neighbor of all is the self. A one-sided reading of the Sermon on the Mount could suggest a disavowal of all self-assertion whatever, the doormat personality. The person who does not claim for himself any education, however, any goods, or any human identity as he grows into personhood, has very little to offer to his neighbor. At the very extreme, he has no real self to share in love with the neighbor. More practically speaking, such a person in our complex world would have no medical or agricultural or business competence nor any material possessions to share with the neighbor. In a world of three billion souls such "saintliness" universalized would require decimating our urban populations for a return to Eden.

Total self-emptying "love" of this sort would reduce personality to a cipher. Its opposite, however, competitive self-aggrandizement at the expense of others, is patently as bad. A Christian ethic proposes wholehearted participation in the ongoing life of the community with the understanding that this life is to be invested on behalf of neighbors-in-community.

In full-bodied loyalty to the near and far neighbors of the human community we shall never be left with the easy conscience—only the forgiven one. It will always be possible to challenge our "solutions" to the dilemmas of near-far responsibility. Any neat system can be challenged as unloving enough.

The affluent suburbanite in a world of need. Our burden is compounded in an age of mass media. We owe neighbor love to the one whose need we see along our path. Daily there is immense and crucial need along our path—famine, the refugees, and the war victims on the front page, the TV screen, and the mailbox appeals. No Christian can finally claim he has done enough for the neighbor so long as he has ten dollars in his bank account and any equity in his home. "What more you need, I will bring you," said the Samaritan. "Do not hoard anxiously against the morrow," says Jesus. "Inasmuch as you have not done it to one of the least of these . . ."

Most suburbanites would not think of themselves as wealthy, although by any standards from history or the Third World they are extremely well-off. Within their immediate community they are good neighbors. "Neighboring" has high priority in suburbia and is relatively easy. Extremes of wealth and poverty are uncommon. The suburbanite does not in his own mind hoard or wastefully consume his means. Should he be well-off, it is bad taste to flaunt his riches. Wealth is best consumed away from the neighbors on expensive vacations, in superb equipment hidden in the stereo or under the hood, or, since further accumulation of wealth is virtually an unquestioned value in our society, in the rich man's numbers game on Wall Street. Radical giving, however, rarely occurs to the suburbanite.

The Christian ethic does not necessarily demand of the suburbanite a vow of poverty for the sake of either far-neighbor need or spiritual self-discipline. Such a vow has been seen as supererogation, beyond the call of duty. We hold those Christians who do adopt such a style in high regard, and we can envy them their freedom of spirit—the followers of Dorothy Day, the rich man inspired by Schweitzer who leaves all to found a hospital in Haiti, the craftsman who, instead of earning more, gives his summer to guide college youths in a work camp or goes into the Peace Corps, the successful businessman who closes up and moves out to a mission field as an administrator on subsistence income. Some denominations maintain counseling offices to help such committed persons find a place of service.

What about the conscience and life-style of the more ordinary Christian who stays behind? We must allow him the freedom to know joy in the good life without a haggling conscience in quest of "right" decisions about distributing his goods and influence. It is essential, however, that Christian faith so challenge and shape this man that he should see all his power and wealth as assets of which he is a steward in the human community. There is no inner circle of people and institutions for whom he can earn and spend and vote while he automatically disregards the claims from other sources—claims upon his wealth and concern.

The word of love is both a command ("Thou shalt love") and an invitation ("That your joy may be complete"). God's word to suburbia is both command and invitation too.

The economic and political resources of suburbia can be used for the near neighbor alone, and suburbia can become richer and "finer" while the cities rot. Or, eschewing such localism, suburbia can become a responsible part of the human community. It would be naïve to believe that this power will be shared without political struggle. It is equally fallacious, however, to think that suburban idealism is useless in evolving new power alignments in the metropolitan social system. The climate of opinion in suburbia is a real part of the struggle through which its strengths will be shared with the society. The Christian doctrine of stewardship, heard and felt in the community, can be an intangible but genuine factor in such a climate of opinion.

Localism in the metropolitan context. To some observers our national history exhibits an alarming movement toward centralism. Conservatives and liberals alike decry the loss of local autonomy. Concurrently in the historical process, however, there have frequently been steps toward local initiative and responsibility. These changes have enabled weaker groups to gain greater control over their own affairs, central authority not having taken those interests adequately into account. Consider the mixed localist-centralist values in two spheres of current metropolitan concern—education and political structure.

1. *Localism and education.* While there has been a long-run trend toward centralizing educational administration, there is now strong pressure in the opposite direction. During the fall of 1968 the struggle over decentralization effectively closed down the massive New York City public school system for three months. Many forces played into the fight—union power and concern for academic freedom and teacher security, urban politics, Black Power demanding an effective voice in a school system that was too ponderous to respond adequately to the racially changing population either in personnel or in teaching. Social theorists favoring decentralization believe that greater neighborhood educational autonomy will help overcome inner-city alienation from the "outsiders'" schools.

Local control of curriculum and staff, which figured so

prominently in the New York dispute, is by no means the only aspect of metropolitan education in which the localist-centralist dilemma figures. Finances are another. Equal opportunity in a technological society has to mean far more for a child than enough to eat and a roof above his head. The tools of life now mean effective literacy and the other kinds of competence necessary to cope in a complex world. Yet inner-city children are provided schools that mean, in Jonathan Kozol's phrase, "Death at an Early Age." Money is a large part of the problem. "Most big city school systems are spending at the absolute limits," writes Robert A. Dentler, Director of the Center for Urban Education. "Per pupil expenditures in surrounding suburbs are, on the average, 30 to 40 percent greater than those in the cities, and capital budgets are even more disparate. . . . State aid has nowhere gone to cities in a way that equalizes expenditures in city and suburb. The gap between poor city and rich suburb has widened yearly from 1956 through 1968." [65] Actually one could readily argue that if the assignment to teach in the inner-city school is tougher, the salaries should not be "equalized" but set higher.

How is a Christian to respond to such a metropolitan concern? He is concerned about the school district close at hand, pays taxes willingly for his school, and belongs to the P.T.A. He takes seriously his responsibilities for his own children. But if he does all that with no concern for the education of children in the inner city, he is victim of the myopia that led the priest and the Levite to pass by on the other side, tending too diligently to their own immediate "responsibilities."

The concerned citizen will favor the centralism that shares resources of rich areas with poor ones through structures of government. Experience with the G.I. Bill and state-financed education systems have proved that outside assistance can be provided in local communities without much interference in local policy. The greater danger in suburbia is that localist arguments will hide an overweening near-neighbor chauvinism that is not concerned enough for the far neighbor in the city schools.

The church has a role in challenging a community to look out for interests of far neighbors as well as near ones. Churches have played a significant part in helping suburban communities face up to opportunities they can offer some children from the inner city through bussing arrangements that bring inner-city children out to the suburbs.[66] In the East, New York, Hartford, Rochester, Boston, and New Haven are among the cities where such a scheme enhances the opportunities for multiracial experience on the part of both suburban children and children from the city. Educators do not presume that the pattern can be duplicated for all ghetto children, but it can be expanded with valuable results. Widespread enforced regionalization of the metropolitan educational process is not politically feasible and would lose the values of localism suggested above. At the same time, action for regional cooperation to counteract racial imbalance and for the purpose of sharing suburban resources more widely with the hardpressed inner-city schools is a moral imperative.

2. *Localism and metropolitan polity.* Robert Wood's books on suburbia rehearse the chaos of "two thousand governments" in greater New York. Waste and stagnation in the face of urgent metropolitan problems result from the existence of 80,000 separate local governmental units across the country, thousands of which could be consolidated. "Across a typical suburban terrain, twenty or thirty or fifty volunteer fire departments buy equipment and with vary-

ing degrees of efficiency put out fires," says Wood. Within
the metropolitan area there are independent school systems, some crammed, some with excess space. "Every census
reports more and smaller—and more self-consciously independent— suburban governments." [67] The Committee for
Economic Development in 1966 recommended an 80 percent reduction in the number of local governing bodies and
a consolidation of jumbled sovereignties into metropolitan
and community units large enough to provide functional
economic bases for the tasks of efficient government.[68]

Suburban governments can become tools by means of
which the suburban ethos asserts an isolationism that
erodes metropolitan well-being. Gans calls suburban government a "defense agency." In a passage worth quoting at
some length, Gibson Winter castigates the provincialism of
suburbia as a "social amnesia" that culminates in its politics:

> There is a deep forgetfulness of our common humanity, for
> the suburb is created as a wall against social differences.
> . . . Suburbia is the protectionist world *par excellence*
> . . . (with) fright and even panic at the thought of racial
> or social class differences in the residential milieu. . . .
>
> The political amnesia of suburbia is perhaps the most
> damaging and corrupting aspect of this degeneration of
> the American hope. . . . We find men and women play-
> ing at small town politics, regretting that the national
> elections do not reflect their conservative hopes, and pre-
> tending that they are being politically responsible. Mean-
> while, these small town politicians work to gain tax advan-
> tages by placing small industries within their tax areas,
> and they maintain low costs for their schools by zoning
> against families who might bring large numbers of chil-
> dren into their communities. These are the politicians who
> scorn metropolitan politics as corrupt; these are the citi-
> zens who clamor for more superhighways and the destruc-
> tion of more central city neighborhoods; these are the pub-

lic-spirited citizenry who rail against public aid and vote down the relief funds which would provide food for under-privileged children. In suburbia the American dream, the hope of fulfillment, degenerates into a conspiracy of public irresponsibility.[69]

Political fragmentation thus not only contributes to economic inefficiency, but to intensified economic inequities of privilege and poverty. To cite the process in one city, the median family income in Detroit rose during the period 1953 to 1959 only 9 percent, from $4400 to $4800. In the suburbs, during this period, the median family income was rising 47 percent, from $4900 to $7200.[70] Moreover, the economic resources of the suburbs around a single city vary so widely that the tax burden of public services is poorly distributed. Cleveland suburbs, for example, showed an assessed per capita valuation (in 1956) varying from $122,-237 in a tiny industrial enclave to $837 in another small piece called Riveredge Township. The larger communities varied from $1858 in Garfield Heights to $4256 in Shaker Heights, the figure for the city itself being $2852.

At the one extreme are the communities which have not sufficient taxable capacity for essential services. The most common case is the bedroom community of low and middle income workers which has little industry or commerce. At the other extreme are the wealthy tax colonies, zoned to keep out low income residents.[71]

Were it still the case that life in a community could be described as self-contained, and that areas of recreation usage, education, culture, and work were more or less coterminous as plotted out on a map, local governments and tax structures floating "on their own bottom" would make far more sense than they do today. As Lyle Fitch says, however,

In the modern metropolitan community a family may re-side in one jurisdiction, earn its living in one or more others, send the children to school in another, and shop and seek recreation in still others. But to a considerable extent, the American local financial system still reflects the presumption that these various activities are concentrated in only one governmental jurisdiction.[72]

Political fragmentation also hinders the coordinated planning that is imperative in metropolitan society. Assuming that the central city needs expressway access to the interstate throughways, which suburb shall it go through? In Massachusetts, a Boston suburb prevented completion of such access for years by exercising its legal powers as an independent jurisdiction. It becomes more and more important that planning designate in advance which areas shall be retained as open space for agricultural and recreational usages and which for residential, industrial, educational, and transportation needs if human activities are not to encroach on each other unnecessarily in demoralizing and destructive ways. Fiercely independent, competitive jurisdictions across the metropolis often resist such reasonable coordination.

Land-use planning in any comprehensive sense does not exist in our larger urban areas. What does exist is a complex game of chess among localities, each attempting to palm off the undesired applicants for space upon their neighboring communities. This is warfare, not planning. . . . (What) is needed for the major urban areas of America is planning which takes cognizance of the land-use needs of the area.[73]

An obvious proposal for counteracting political provincialism and economic inequities in metropolis is the amalgamation of all these little governments into one.

With its uni-gov program, Indianapolis has recently merged with surrounding Marion County to become one political unit, a major step of responsible politics. That metropolitan government is the wave of the near future is to be doubted, however. This and other steps somewhat like it (Dade County, Florida, and Seattle, Washington) have not been widely copied. Moreover, at the present stage of racial change in American urban life, a move toward metropolitan government could be a serious setback to Negro progress. In many northern cities the black population is fast approaching a 50 percent level, and political organization in the ghetto is becoming a reality that is yielding dividends in terms both of reducing alienation among blacks and of establishing greater social justice in the opportunities and services offered by city hall. The 1968 elections of black mayors in Gary, Indiana, and in Cleveland are two cases in point. Annexation of a ring of white suburbs would set this process back by putting together again a white coalition of dominating proportions.[74]

Proposals of metropolitan government must always be balanced by a consideration of values served by a localist emphasis. Constantinos Doxiadis, the brilliant architect and planner, urges us to keep in mind what he calls the "human scale" as we plan our homes or public buildings, our subways, and our neighborhoods. Man must not be belittled by the design of his environment or by the speed with which he sees himself move through it, if this can be prevented. Similar arguments could be applied to the structures of government.[75] Jane Jacobs in her influential book on city life and city planning [76] proposed that many functions of New York City administration be decentralized to district governments for areas incorporating about a hundred thousand people each to facilitate access to government. In the large metropolis services in matters relating to traffic, sanitation, law enforcement, education, recreation, building codes, and welfare are presently administered from such a distance that citizen access is difficult, or, if decentralized, they are not related to each other in what ought to be a neighborhood city hall. As a result the citizen's participation in government is restricted in fact as well as in his "feel" for his city. It is not surprising that the call for "ombudsmen" to stand on the citizen's side as a watchdog against state and city governments is growing.

In the light of this mix of advantages and disadvantages in present metropolitan polity, what proposals can the responsible suburban churchman support? There is little doubt that better structures reflecting the mutual interdependence of all the jurisdictions within the metropolis should be encouraged. Indianapolis shows us an important direction, but even short of that other programs merit our attention. Just as in UN agencies on the international level, although actual "federal" unification into world government is presently impossible, piecemeal steps of cooperation help to build responsible community. Added to cooperation in the educational field, there are many other private and public efforts to be encouraged: suburban participation in the United Fund, systems for sharing federal and state tax revenues with hard-pressed cities, state recreational facilities instead of restricted suburban ones, ad hoc units like transit authorities, and regional planning offices. The latter are increasingly effective by virtue of veto powers over certain federal subsidies to cities and towns within their area.

Localism and the churches. The church well knows the localist-centralist tension. Bringing "government" close to the people has been the rationale of "local autonomy" in the traditions with congregational polity: Baptist, Disciples, and Congregationalist. Theologically this localism was understood to free the Holy Spirit and maintain over the congregation the Lordship of Christ rather than "church power" of presbyter, bishop, and king. On the other hand, localism in church polity has repeatedly been corrupted by faulty and isolationist deviation in doctrine and mission. The virtue of presbyterianism and episcopacy has been its tangible representation of wholeness in the body of Christ and a countervailing balance to localist self-centeredness. The responsible suburban church must see itself as one member of the whole body, a branch on the vine, and give attention to the practical manner in which this wholeness is embodied in denominational and ccumenical affairs. The rich church and the poor church are one in Christ. Money shared from the one to the other for mission program in the inner city is not charity, but, as Paul said of the offering from Corinth for the famine victims in Jerusalem (far neighbors indeed in that day), "It is a question of equality" (II Cor. 8:14, NEB).

In its enthusiasm for secular mission, the suburban church should beware of overlooking parishes of the inner city. The National Conference of Black Churchmen in 1967 appealed to white churches to work through ghetto churches in their mission rather than starting programs of their own. Suburban churches too easily write off black inner-city congregations on the basis of stereotypes, especially those congregations outside their own denomination. By doing so, they distance themselves from the majority of blacks in churches. (Ninety-five percent of the Negroes in Washington, D.C., were found to belong to church groups outside the main-line denominations.) They also accept a stereotype that is often wrong. A black Pentecostal store-front congregation near my home, for example, is served by a capable woman who has had but four years of formal education. Yet she and the congregation operate an "annex" for evicted families, and for young people from the rural South who can get a good start in the city with the help of "Mother Wheeler," the pastor. Black ministers of minor denominations are developing a political consciousness that belies their pietistic heritage. Stronger ecumenical structures can strengthen the church as one of the most significant links that tie the wider metropolis together.

In its internal program, the responsible suburban church will preach and teach mutual interdependence with the city. The message, "love your neighbor," finally gets through to people when it results in concrete decisions—in this case for metropolitan cooperation. Should annexation of an unincorporated edge-of-city development be proposed, for example, the only issues to be weighed are not lower insurance rates and higher tax bills, but moral issues also—citizen responsibility for the urban neighbor.

Teaching even young suburban children about the city of which they are indirectly a part is an opportunity for Christian education. One suburban church sponsored a day-long bus trip during a school vacation; on the tour they included visits to the chaplain in the city hospital, to a church social service center, to the day care center in one housing project and to a library in another (both church initiated), and to a newly rehabilitated house to be resold by a church-sponsored nonprofit housing corporation. A confirmation class canceled its weekly session at the church in favor of a group trip to a civil rights rally.

The congregation's consideration of its own civic behavior can become a dramatic process of moral reflection and growth. More and more frequently, congregations and other nonprofit institutions are making gifts to city governments in lieu of taxes; a reasonable amount is that proportion of the real estate tax, which, if there were one levied on the church property, would represent fire protection, police costs, and such other public services as are "consumed" by the congregation. Parsonages and manses in most suburban congregations no longer represent housing maintained "for the convenience of the employer"; real estate and income taxes should be paid on this portion of the minister's "salary" as by any other professional.

Through strategies of community organization the suburban congregation can counteract the natural feeling of being cut off from metropolitan life. We will discuss this aspect of suburban action in Chapter IV, Section 2.

A serious call. Clearly, the kind of metropolitan concern we have considered in this chapter is not in the simple self-interest of the suburb. It asks the suburb, instead of fighting against the city, to invest its strength alongside it for the sake of metropolitan well-being. This is not unrealistic idealism. Project Concern advocates have successfully argued suburbia's moral responsibility for the city and, on a small scale, ghetto children were bussed to better schools. So have proponents of moderate-income housing input for suburban neighborhoods. As the "we" community is extended beyond parochial borders, far neighbors become near ones and John Q. Public is ready to consider small steps that help make the whole city a community.

We have not proposed a vow of poverty for the Christian suburbanite, but Christian faith entails responsibility as well as a freedom from burdensome legalism. Life with the forgiven conscience involves the disciplines of love. James Forman's first half-billion dollar figure for "reparation" contributions by churches was not implausible if the recent new giving by a 1500-member Berkeley church could be widely duplicated—$96,000 for a Reconciliation Fund for black community development.

Long ago, William Law wrote *A Serious Call to the Devout and Holy Life;* the Christian gospel addresses to suburbia a serious call as well, a call to share its wealth and political power with the metropolitan community. Few are the persons or communities who do not think themselves hard-pressed enough that it is difficult to cut back in lifestyle or make room for the needy stranger, even in this rich age. A serious call to suburban stewardship challenges us to see the far neighbor in metropolis for his need and to recognize our suburban affluence for what it is.

What does Christian stewardship mean for Jack and Mary Browning in Bellevue Acres or Cloverdale? Does it not imply a bias toward simplicity on the part of comfortable suburban Christians, a readiness to yield up privilege in political and economic structures if such a change will build a richer life for the whole urban community? James Gustafson raises such a question in reviewing the position of those ethicists who see in Christ a pattern for the moral life:

> Does the following of Jesus as moral ideal require that one dress as men did in Judea and Galilee? Obviously no. But does the picture of Jesus require that the follower of Jesus dress simply, without expensive adornment, without luxury? Is simplicity in manner and style of life the proper inference for those who would follow one who had no place to lay his head? . . . If it is, the Christian moral ideal in our time would run . . . strongly against the cultural and economic stream which presses more and more consumer goods into life, without regard for simplicity, not to mention self-denial.[77]

Gustafson then quotes Bonhoeffer: "If there is no element of asceticism in our lives . . . we shall find it hard to train for the service of Christ."

At the very least, an asceticism that must be preached in suburban America acknowledges that suburbia cannot live to itself and die to itself. It cannot with a localist rationalization bask in its own affluence disdainful of the far-near neighbors of the inner city and the nations beyond the seas. From Philippians, the *kenōsis* or self-emptying of Christ has become a model for a kenotic church and a kenotic Christian posture: "Have this mind among yourselves, which you have in Christ Jesus, who, though he was in the form of God, did not count equality with God a thing to be grasped, but emptied himself, taking the form of a servant" (ch. 2:5-7). Our serious call is that suburbia and suburbanites turn outward from their enclaves to employ their political power and collective wealth to help the whole metropolis take on more marks of the city of God.

IV | Strategies for Metropolitan Mission

Introduction

We have laid down two matrices for reflection on suburban ministry. The first looked at the suburbanite himself— the life situations of youth, and of suburban men and women in their productive years. The second examined three social issues that bear upon suburbia today. We now reflect upon styles of ministry, strategies of mission. We cut through the pudding in another dimension to discover elements that we missed before.

1. VOLUNTARISM

One of the fastest growing movements in main-line churches as this book is written is an organization called "Fish." Taking its name from one of the oldest Christian symbols, Fish exemplifies a common approach to church mission beyond internal parish activities. First organized in the Anglican Church of St. Andrew's, Oxford, England, the Fish pattern was copied in West Springfield, Massachusetts, in 1964, under the leadership of an Episcopal rector, Robert L. Howell.

Fish is a free emergency service that can be reached at all times through a telephone-answering service. Typical examples of assistance offered by Fish volunteers are transportation, baby-sitting, hot meals brought in. In the scores of communities where Fish is now present, mass media inform the public that there is such lay volunteer help available in emergencies. In one typical program, a volunteer is a person who offers a day a month to serve as a telephone coordinator, to be available for transportation, to prepare a few meals, and the like. Some careful planning, an answering service, a corps of trained coordinators, and a larger number of willing volunteers are about all that is necessary to launch this local, nonprofessional, neighborly service, one that is deeply satisfying to the participants.

Fish illustrates both the strengths and the limitations of voluntarism. This approach to church mission is one of the oldest and most characteristic manifestations of Christian concern. There is not a serious-minded Christian congregation in which voluntarism is not practiced. Voluntarism means uncoerced individual help to others—a casserole delivered to the neighbor family when the homemaker is in the hospital, a pair of ice skates given by a businessman to a boy in the Scout troop he leads. In city after city voluntarism is organized on a sizable basis through the churches. In San Diego, California, it is the primary cooperative activity of 31 Presbyterian churches that jointly employ a full-time coordinator of mission to the city. In a New England suburb, a steel executive and his wife led a Bible Study group in an inner-city housing project for thirteen years—until a resident minister was installed in the area. During the '60s, tens of thousands of high school and college students were involved in tutoring younger children who had educational handicaps of some sort. Under OEO grants in some cities and on a volunteer basis in others, meals are arranged for the elderly in housing projects and individual homes, and meal companions can be arranged for the homebound.

In a Virginia community, a hundred men and women volunteers make useful articles for the Arlington Child Development Center—toys, work benches, doll houses, and doll clothes. Through arrangements with a prison chaplain's office in Massachusetts, up to three hundred men "outmates" per week have been involved in visits to inmates for purposes of conversation, rehabilitation, and possible assistance in getting a new start upon parole. WICS—Women in Community Services, a nationwide interfaith organization of women's church groups—has helped screen thousands of young women for the Women's Job Corps. One City Mission Society supervises several hundred volunteers each year, the standard for the volunteer being the giving of time at least once a week. The First Presbyterian Church of Berkeley, California, has 350 trained volunteers at the core of its mission program, organized with the help of a minister of outreach; these volunteers engage in programs of adult literacy, counseling and referral for personal and family needs, Big Brother help for boys, job training, youth outreach in a hippie community.[78]

"What are you doing in the church this year?" I asked Ivan, a suburbanite metallurgical engineer who willingly assumed heavy responsibilities in the congregation. "Well, I am teaching a Sunday school class, but let me tell you something else I'm working on. John (a welding equipment salesman) and I have persuaded my boss to open the shop a night a week and we're training ten men from the ghetto as skilled welders. These aren't exactly the hard core, I suppose, but half of them are unemployed and half earning very little. The motivation is amazing—100 percent attendance, excitement about the work. I can guarantee them jobs at $3.50 to $5.00 an hour as soon as they finish."

These ten men were recruited through the Opportunities Industrialization Center (OIC), a black self-help job-training organization to be found now in many metropolitan centers. This is voluntarism, and Ivan is right when he says that this is his primary "church work" for the present.

First among the advantages of the voluntaristic approach to church mission is the fact that it is a person-to-person ministry. Voluntarism can involve large numbers of people in humanizing life of the metropolitan world. In the "two cultures" of metropolis, we segregate ourselves by social status, occupation, residence, and race, but the face-to-face situations of voluntarism always carry the possibility of trust and compassion that can transcend such social barriers.

In a discussion among several people from the inner city, one a former prostitute, another a former alcoholic who had led a desperate and chaotic life, the most salient feature of the stories on how these two and others had found strength for a better life was the fact that someone had cared and helped in a personal way—a social worker in one case, a nun in another. No matter what the extent of material comfort and programmed welfare aid, the *diakonia* of persons in concerned service to one another will always be in demand. In this day of the nuclear family, mutual assistance that was once provided by extended kinship groups is evaporating. Voluntaristic aid is not solely directed toward lower-income groups and their problems. Fish calls come as often from middle-class homes as from poverty and minority groups.

Secondly, voluntarism moves inevitably in an ecumenical direction. Once people reach beyond the congregation in service, human need and goodwill rather than religious tradition define the natural associations. Fish began with Episcopalians in Springfield, but it very early became an ecumenical project as it moved across the country—embracing Catholics, Methodists, Presbyterians, Jews, etc. It matters little which kind of person is at the wheel when the main concern of driver and passenger is to get that man to the hospital to see his wife.

Thirdly, voluntarism is a tangible outlet for concern and talent. The human spirit craves concrete expression for even its deepest and most "spiritual" intentions. Voluntarism opens the way for the specific participation that we need. Martin Luther King's 1955 campaign in Montgomery, Alabama, gave people with clear grievances the chance to "vote with their feet." Abbé Michonneau,[79] an insightful Paris priest, says that there is a mass element in religion; his festive parades gave everyone in the neighborhood an avenue for participation—marching or cheering. Voluntarism offers a way to participate in more than spectator religion.

Moreover, voluntarism as a tangible act completes the cycle of penitence and concern. Said one minister,[80] "to load people up with guilt and give them no handle to deal with the problem only makes them fearful and reactionary." "We need specific outlets to help us show the substance of faith in our lives," says a Fish leader. Voluntarism is an important step beyond checkbook charity. To the vast majority of Christians in church pews, denominational strategy for social amelioration is distant and intangible. Our social action strategy needs to bring the individual an experience of his own involvement in efforts at social change.

Voluntarism is not by itself an adequate or complete program of social engagement by the churches, but it is an important part of that engagement. As one urban strategist puts it: "In helping our churches get into action on the crisis of the cities, we need and can find something for everybody. All kinds of help, tame and radical, are legitimate."

Remarkable resources often appear as voluntarism develops. Supplementary music education programs for inner-city schools, for example, have been staffed and equipped by volunteers in several cities. Professionally and as hobbyists, successful suburbanites make movies, cut records, build or operate complicated electronic equipment, teach athletic skills, work in the visual arts. Shared through voluntarism, all these skills may become a "sacrament" of human community.

Fourthly, voluntarism, properly supervised, has educational value. It is the primary contact for thousands of suburbanites with the reality of poverty and wide income discrepancies. "It's changed people's lives to go see those shacks" reported one minister. "Even the very conservative sorts, who used to feel that people who are down and out are there because of laziness, begin to get some other ideas." [81] Feedback to the congregation will acquaint the suburban congregation with some realities of life in the "other America." Voluntarism can lead to social action by providing a closer look at social problems.

Finally, voluntaristic service expresses the pastoral dimension of ministry on the part of the church in the world. It points to the love of a caring God. The ordained minister is best regarded as a coach who helps all members in their ministry rather than as the sole practitioner of pastoral care. No emphasis in the ecclesiology of the past decade is stronger than that upon the ministry of the laity.

Many human needs that were once left to the pastor will be effectively met by the neighborly concern of sensitive people in the congregation.[82]

It is no less important to recognize the pitfalls in church voluntarism. The first danger is paternalism. The volunteer can receive two kinds of satisfaction. He has been of use, has learned something, and has met another person to share life with him. This is good. On the other hand, his service may simply reinforce a pride that knows no humility or penitence. Paternalism is an insidious component of charity whenever there is such pride in the giver. The volunteer needs to acknowledge that his strength for giving is not his own doing; in an ultimate sense this is simply a sharing of life between equals.

As in the company towns of an earlier industrial era, the worst evil done by paternalistic charity is the emasculation of the recipient, who is maintained in dependency. For just this reason, the analogy of colonialism is legitimately invoked in the rhetoric of those who crusade for welfare reform. Insightful coordinators of volunteer activity stress the two-way nature of the volunteer's relationship; unless the outer city comes to recognize that the inner city has strengths to offer, that the outer city must learn as well as serve, its service will be corrupted by paternalism. Middle-class people may learn from the inner city a certain toughness in coping with life as it comes, a freedom of spirit that will put uptight suburbanites to shame, spontaneity and steadiness of religious faith, communal generosity, and a valuable realism about human sin and social structures. A suburban pastor, reacting to the experiences of joint efforts with an urban church said, "We are not physical out here. We're terribly limited in our range of experience. We are time-bound and lack spontaneity."

Paternalism is as much an institutional problem as a hazard in person-to-person relationships. One ordained urban activist for the churches, David Simpson in Danbury, Connecticut, writes it this way:

> We are not at all interested in creating another do-good agency which seeks to salve its conscience by doing something for the disadvantaged. . . . Poverty is much more an attitude, a psychological reaction to a situation, than it is a lack of money. Services rendered only serve to reinforce conviction that the recipient is helpless, hopeless, and indeed inferior. . . .
>
> We are more interested in helping ghetto residents to develop the leadership whereby they can solve their own problems than we are in solving their problems for them.

Even the best programs of voluntarism always skirt the edge of paternalism, and every program of this sort must reflect again and again the insight and programmatic goal represented by Simpson's words.

Another hazard in voluntarism is complacency. It is easy for the volunteer who enters upon service with the feeling that his work will accomplish great good and then discovers the tough persistence of personality problems and social ills to feel "I've done my bit," and fail to continue in the penitence and hope that are affectional grounds of Christian love. Voluntarism can serve to breed the easy conscience that no longer sees God's judgment upon the differentials in income, opportunity, and power that account for needless deprivation of human life.

Voluntary action may provide enough satisfaction and achieve enough results that, coupled with complacency, it blinds enthusiasts to the need for structural social change. The National Alliance of Businessmen, for example, was reported to have put more than 100,000 hard-core unemployed onto business payrolls in 1968, and it would be tempting, therefore, to think that the private sector could solve this problem. Economists and business leaders, however, stepping back to study the programs, stressed the limits of what private enterprises can be expected to do. They underscored the need for expanded governmental programs to meet some of the basic problems.[83] Structural change would tackle the problems of urban education and basic economic inequity. Voluntarism is usually an after-the-fact approach to social ills, a "Band-aid." Preventive medicine and deep surgery may be more to the point.

Voluntarism needs sensitive leadership and cannot be presented with messianic enthusiasm as the whole expression of Christian concern in society. Nonetheless, voluntarism is one of the best opportunities for suburban church mission, for it is one of the most viable ways of mobilizing the vast resources of suburbia for the common good.

2. COMMUNITY ORGANIZATION

People Against Racism. Allies for Urban Progress. Metropolitan Area Coalition. Simply to list names for the numerous alliances through which churches are attacking urban issues reveals a second strategy for metropolitan mission.

Community organization was long a branch of social work, but it has been given new and controversial connotations by the work of Saul Alinsky and his Industrial Areas Foundation.[84] The urban neighborhoods organized by Alinksy, and by others like him, have sought to meet various needs through building organization—a reduction of exploitation or neglect by the political establishment and business firms, the counteraction of various social forces that feed on and destroy an urban area where there is a power vacuum. They have wanted to prevent block-busting in the transition neighborhood, to reverse destructive renewal plans, or to gain a voice in industrial employment policy. Black people work for larger voice in governing their neighborhoods. Mexicans fight for unions and a living wage in the cities and fields of the Southwest.

Community organization has become a major element in church efforts at human renewal in the city. Hundreds of thousands of dollars of church funds (Catholic, Protestant, and Jewish) have been invested in the work of organizers hired from Alinsky's IAF alone. The Interreligious Foundation for Community Organization (IFCO) recently established, raised nearly $1,000,000 in its first year of operation with about a dozen denominations giving the primary support. Understanding and interpreting all of this is itself a challenge to suburban church leadership, for funds contributed to denominational mission sometimes come back to the city and organize opposition to the very institutions in which the suburban contributors participate.

Beyond supporting programs in the central city, however, suburban communities themselves are now organizing. Alinsky is turning the efforts of the IAF to training organizers, half of whom are being coached in a middle-class suburban context.

One reason for suburban community organization is that the urban poor need political and financial allies. The poor are now a minority in this country and cannot with the power of their ballots alone accomplish another social shift like that of the New Deal. This is one of Alinsky's most frequent arguments to radicals who think to go it alone in social reform without concern for the middle-class liberal. Only an alliance of white liberals with the blacks and the poor can win in the political process. Michael Harrington suggests that several sectors of the population are ready to join such a coalition, among them the liberal wing of labor, new white-collar groups such as union-organized technicians and engineers, scientists, educators, medical personnel, and liberal Catholic insurgents.

Rochester's Friends of FIGHT was an early example of a strong suburban ally for a militant ghetto organization. With the help of denominational money and Alinsky organizers, FIGHT (Freedom, Integration, God, Honor, Today) was founded in the wake of the severe Rochester riots in 1964. FIGHT's most publicized success was its confrontation with Kodak, but the organization won other victories too—an increase in the number of dwellings to be built by the urban renewal agency along with a policy that some new building must precede demolition, and better city services must be rendered to the ghetto. Observers also report that FIGHT has served as a catalyst for the white community, however, creating a tide for change. Churches, embroiled in controversy because of objections to denominational funding of FIGHT organizers, have had to reflect on the city's needs and church mission. Friends of FIGHT developed as a white suburban group. Through patient, steady commitment Friends developed a trust relationship with the activist blacks. FIGHT was initiator, but Friends was a resource. It provided information through contacts in the white community, information to which FIGHT did not have easy access. It provided money by winning support for FIGHT in many groups of suburbia. It encouraged moral support in the wider white community through interpretation of the community organization process.

The other reason for community organization in the suburbs is not unlike that for the inner city. Suburban communities themselves may experience the handicaps of poor organization for constructive community action. Suburbia often suffers a trivialized political life. This is epitomized by the story of one suburban mayor who had to stay in office long after he wanted to retire since his term had ended, because no one else thought enough of the job to run.

Suburban political structures are often inadequate to cope with the strong forces of urbanization, forces that demand coordination and planning if maximum human welfare is to be served. Without strong government and adequate community coherence, a developing suburb may sacrifice one or another of the following by default: control of shopping-center development, rational traffic patterns, good schools, protection of open space and parkland, clean water and air, adequate library and recreational resources, aesthetic appeal, and responsible interrelationship with the central city.

The philosophy of the community organizer most typically involves getting people together around their own felt needs. Self-interest is a rule of thumb for Alinsky, so vigorously pressed that his philosophy evokes opposition from others who believe exploitation of self-interest is an illegitimate tactic. The better organizers in the suburbs, however, are not actually exploiting the narrowest self-interest of the suburb. The reactionary suburbanite is not recruited, and those with a broader understanding of the community's needs are, so there are broader "self-interests." With the organization of one community around the need for teen-age recreation facilities, another around concern for education, and another around the need for open housing, these groups would have the appearance of such diversity as to be of little use in overall metropolitan strategy, but the net effect is to fill an organizational vacuum, and if the community organizations are linked even loosely, they provide the basis on which coordinated metropolitan-wide efforts can take shape.

Following this philosophy in interchurch cooperation in the Greater Washington area, coordinator David J. Robb says, "Our emphasis is not upon relating suburban and inner city churches directly but in building up a network of 'group ministries' both in the city and in the suburban areas, all directing their focus upon their own community, and relating their work to an overall metropolitan strategy which each component will help to shape."

In Detroit, ten Suburban Action Centers are projected alongside four community organization centers in the city. Each is to be manned by clergy, one released for at least a year for full-time organizing work, another from a different faith group (Catholic or Protestant or Jewish) for part-time service as his assistant. The projected budget for the program in 1970 was $650,000. The suburban organizations center on local needs as seen by the people of good will. In relating to central-city blacks Suburban Action takes a far more activist approach than the "getting to know Negroes" emphasis of a bygone day. Effective organization and institutions in the white community is the goal, organization to change those oppressive conditions under which black people live.

Some suburban community organization has taken a direct clue from the Kerner Report and its charge of white racism. Using the name of a national group, and staff leadership employed by a Council of Churches, groups in seventeen suburbs around Waterbury, Connecticut, are aligning themselves as People Against Racism. Says one of their documents:

We have the potential to establish a power base in suburban towns to change the laws that wall out the Black and the Poor. We have the potential to introduce and support legislation that will improve life and conditions in the city. Black pressure groups are forming, but they need a white counterpart if real community change is to take place. If we are to make any dent at all in white racism and if we are to make any impact on the social evils of our society it will require a broad and deep organization of whites.

Rev. Roger Floyd, effective coordinator of this effort, has had inner-city experience in rent strikes and open-housing campaigns. He believes many of the same strategies for action can be moved to the suburbs.

The place of the church in supporting community organization is too little understood in the pulpits and pews of suburbia. Richard C. Cornuelle provides valuable perspective on this issue in material that was quoted by a national church group as they proposed a new effort in urban mission policy.

Overwhelmed by the problems of the Depression, we suddenly turned most of our attention to Washington. In so doing, we unconsciously turned our backs on the tradition of non-governmental action which had held our dream together for 150 years.

It quickly became fashionable to speak of American life in terms of two "sectors": the public sector, which is a prejudicial euphemism for government, and the private sector, which is profit-seeking commerce. We leave out the third sector in our national life, the one which is neither governmental nor commercial. We ignore the institutions which once played such a decisive part in the society's vibrant growth. By assuming a major role in meeting public needs, thus leaving less to government, this third sector once made it possible for us to build a humane society and a free society together.

This important third force deserves a name. It is a distinct identifiable part of American life, not just a misty area between commerce and government. I have come to call it "the independent sector." [85]

Cornuelle, of course, is making the same emphasis as de Tocqueville did when he noted the voluntaristic initiative so important in American society. An independent sector emphasis capitalizes on our voluntaristic tradition. It stresses the value of social organization outside business and government. Much of the weight in better literature from the student and political left reflects the same voluntaristic theme.

The church is a very logical instrument for much of the rebuilding of community strength. Church institutions have a long history as centers of community life. The church already has personnel recruited in its ordained ministry and its committed laymen. As a religious institution, it relates social renewal to a framework that has personal and moral meaning, a framework that can motivate people for social action and prevent overzealous moralistic judgment upon those who oppose particular reforms.

A cooperative parish on the north side of Chicago illustrates the development of community strength through an alliance of churches. The Northside Cooperative Ministry (NSCM) is an organization of two dozen churches of eight denominations along with a neighborhood house, an arts foundation, a coffeehouse, and a college student community. Growing out of typical activities in voluntarism, which were projects either of NSCM collectively or of individual congregations within it—tutoring, a daycamp for children, a coffeehouse, Meals on Wheels for shut-ins—a more activist approach evolved, and effective task forces on education, civil rights, housing, and peace were organized to mobilize the strength of that Northside district in Chicago. "Our major priority," said David Deering, the co-ordinator of the NSCM churches and agencies, "is to help the whole community develop its own programs and to develop occasions and structures for the unheard people to voice their own needs." [86] Similar area parishes are as viable in the suburbs. In North Arlington, Virginia, six churches took the name of North Arlington Parish and united all their efforts, except worship and religious education, launching Fish and other forms of voluntarism soon after the Parish began.

Deering's understanding of social action by the churches is not unlike the "advocate planning" style that church leaders have adopted elsewhere. Believing that people do not have enough voice in policies that affect them when all they do is attend hearings on renewal plans initiated at city hall level, certain neighborhoods have been helped to hire their own consultants so that they could come to city authorities with their own hopes and wishes carefully and competently defended. They have their own "advocate" just as the accused has his at court.

As a very important part of the "independent sector" in American life, the church has certain theological and empirical resources that are particularly relevant to community organization strategy. Because it acknowledges that all men are sinners, Christian doctrine leads us to favor social structures that provide a check upon the power of every dominant group lest, thinking itself wholly virtuous, it tyrannize or infantilize another. Therefore, for example, when church money helps an inner-city community organization that ends up contesting the "Establishment" whose members contributed the funds in the first place, church funds might be expected to stick it out longer than those from political sources. Such has been the case.

Secondly, the church has grass-roots contact upon which it can capitalize in making its contribution to the urban community. Pastors in both suburbs and the inner city are close to the people and can help them express their needs. Ministers represent a tradition that is now being used by public agencies. The job description of a "neighborhood worker" under an OEO program, for example, is very similar to the job descriptions inner-city ministers have used for years, except that it leaves out Sunday morning worship. While training community mental health workers a medical leader said they should work in the community "like ministers."

Thirdly, in spite of the limitations on all voluntary associations, there is yet a certain independence for the church, a freedom for action unavailable to such groups as United Fund agencies. The church is not the possession of a commercial enterprise or a political machine. In most denominations the local congregation has more independence than a branch bank or a chain store would have. It can institute changes without checking the opinion downtown in the main offices.

At the same time, a church is related to people from other parts of the city. Gibson Winter has seen in the church a resource for communication across the city's divisions of geography, social class, and economic interest. "The ministry of reconciliation of the servant church is the restoration of communication to society," he says.[87] Cultivating awareness of the ways they fit into this metropolitan communications grid is a major responsibility for suburban churches.

Good community life doesn't just happen when people move into houses or towns near one another. It is built through organization. Depending on the strength of its community life, suburbia may remain a mere agglomeration of houses poorly planned and victimized by the forces of urban sprawl, or it may become a viable human settlement, better serving not only its own people but indirectly the metropolitan areas as a whole. Suburban community organization initiated or encouraged by churches is one significant step toward that end.

3. SYSTEMS AND MODELS

The secret of the DNA molecule was unraveled when scientists learned better how to look at it—in this case with X-rays. Similarly, successful work with people and institutions is often a matter of perspective. This chapter proposes further productive ways of looking at church mission in the city.

Mission to Sectors

In engineering and the social sciences a currently popular and useful adjustment of perspective is called systems analysis.

Systems analysis typically does at least the following:
1. It concentrates on the process and structures that create a problem.
2. It takes account of how different systems affect each other and how an answer to one problem may create difficulties in another system.
3. It proposes several alternative models that might meet the problem and it employs an "input-output" or "cost-benefit" analysis to help choose among them.

4. In launching pilot or prototype action, it builds in a feedback mechanism that will facilitate the modification of erroneous proposals.

A systems analysis of the city in relation to the church suggests a new mapping process for mission. As we look at the people of the metropolis and think of the church, we ordinarily map the city geographically and distribute churches across the diagram (see facing page).

An analysis of metropolis by systems would require a "map" of another sort. Antipoverty programs, for example, have studied the handicaps suffered by the poor in terms of access to systems of education, recreation, housing, health, and employment. The resulting strategy is designed to increase the opportunity for the poor in each of these areas.

Likewise, when reflecting on church mission it is useful to hold in mind a systems or sector "map" of metropolis to supplement an image derived from geography alone. One of the more widely circulated diagrams of this sort was prepared by Stanley Hallett, for the planning office of the Church Federation of Chicago. Modifying and simplifying it a bit, we can view the city as a set of systems represented in the pie-shaped pieces on page 148. The mass media, as Hallett suggests, are drawn as a background system relating the various primary sectors to one another.

As this diagram to chart the life of the city is used, one crucial question for the church in the modern metropolis readily appears. How is the church to be present in these sectors of human life? How is it to prompt moral reflection in law and commerce and education? How do we put the steeples on this kind of map?

The churchman who holds in mind this second concept of the city easily recognizes his Christian vocation to be far more than his attendance at a geographical point on Sun-

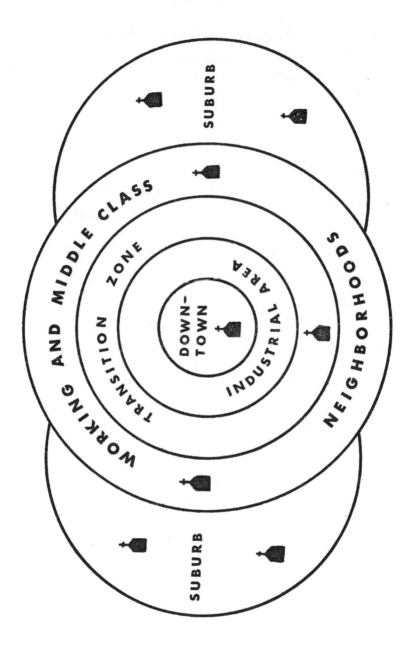

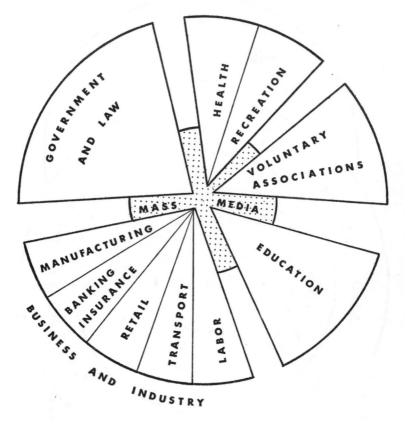

day morning. He sees himself investing Christian concern in those sectors where he is involved at work and in his avocational pursuits. He is the one who makes the "church" present on this second map. One insightful layman, chairing a major city commission appointed after the summer riots of 1967, was asked why the church was not represented on the committee; the questioner had expected to find a minister or a priest present. "But we are all in the church," said the chairman. "The church *is* represented."

As a map of metropolis this analysis challenges us to create new forms of ministry on behalf of the church. We have a mission in these sectors. For example, Rev. Robert Forsberg of Wider City Parish in New Haven, Connecticut, sees himself primarily as a minister in the educational sector. The laymen associated with Forsberg in ministry include parents, working for better educational support from the city and state government, and school personnel, who are responding to the crisis in urban education. There is a ministry of reconciliation in this sector just as in the parish community. Conflicting parent and student groups need to be helped to communicate with one another. Grass-roots feeling among inner-city people needs to reach middle-class professionals, interpretation in the other direction needs improvement. There is a prophetic function to be served—challenging the public to invest more concern in education and challenging the educational bureaucracy with new ideas for improving its schools and its teaching. The suburbanite schoolteacher or administrator, participating in a "church" in his work sector, will discover perspective and sensitivity for his own professional service as a Christian. The parish church can only rarely address his work directly, and all too often his own routine professional relationships do not offer much direct encouragement, either.

Hospital and university chaplaincies are ideally placed for sector ministries. They have but to use a wide-angle lens and look beyond their narrower, more traditional role in pastoral care of individual persons.

Sector ministries elsewhere are multiplying. Industrial Missions are being established. Metropolitan Associates of Philadelphia has organized groups of laymen within each of six sectors of urban life and work: politics and government, business and industry, education and culture, social and community organizations, medicine and health, physical planning. Downtown churches in some cities are seeing businessmen's lunch groups as potential loci of sector ministry.

The systems "map" of the city helps interpret to laymen the often-puzzling phenomenon of "new forms" of the ministry and the increasing number of theologically trained students who move from seminary to assignments other than the parish church. It is wholly reasonable that in a medium-sized town, instead of deploying thirty-five professional leaders into parishes as pastors, plus one to a church council and one to a campus ministry, the churches should establish a different ratio. Thirty parish leaders and five or ten paraparochial professionals would make more sense in terms of systems analysis of the city. We have already shifted farther in this direction than many churchmen realize. A recent count in one denomination, the United Church of Christ, shows that besides the 5,366 pastors and associate ministers, there are 1,626 other ordained ministers deployed by the church, only 350 of whom are in the denominational bureaucracy. An additional 272 were reported in business or other secular vocations; some hard thinking and more experimentation should enable at least some of these men to utilize their theological training as "worker-priests" in sector ministries where they are employed.

As a first step in the direction of sector ministry a local church can consider "seconding" or designating a portion of one staff member's time to a specific nonparish role. One New England suburban church took on a new assistant minister with the specific assignment of spending at least one day of his work week in the inner city, working with black churches there and discovering the needs of the area in which his availability or his contacts in a white middle-class suburb might prove to be of use. Another listed as one of five parts of a job description, "developing Faith Church Bridge Builders, enabling the church to become involved in ministry to the inner city."

A more dramatic deployment of professional staff by a local church is to be found in Rockville, Maryland. Two new neighboring suburban churches, one Presbyterian, one United Church of Christ, found themselves struggling with buildings to pay for and the inefficient use of staff. Merger created a viable 700-member congregation. One minister now serves in the traditional way; the second is designated "Community Minister." The latter directs a Center for Community Ministries, promotes ecumenical and volunteer activities, and relates himself and many lay people to various public problems in the town.

Employing a minister to the public sector is difficult for a single parish, but such an assignment on behalf of a group of congregations is not at all farfetched. In Eliot Church, Newton, Massachusetts, a minister of education, Charles Harper, was about to resign when the imaginative senior pastor, Harold R. Fray, Jr., proposed that since the church was in less need of a minister of education, it should sponsor a new ministry through the same staff member.[88] After a year's study, Cooperative Metropolitan Ministries came into being, a project supported by several suburban churches as an arm of their metropolitan ministry. (By 1968 there were twenty-three churches supporting CMM: three Roman Catholic, three Jewish temples, the rest Protestant; four in central Boston, the rest in the suburbs.)

CMM's primary area of activity is that of low- and moderate-income housing at the present. The program moves in other directions as well, however—personal, financial, or consultative assistance to the South End family relocation program, Mothers for Adequate Welfare, VISTA, United South End Settlements, Council for Public Schools, and the Opportunities Industrialization Center. Through this ministry the suburban churches have had an avenue of relationship to urban education community organization and problems of employment and youth.

In their own ways the Rockville and Eliot Churches represent a systems analysis of the work of the church in the world. Staff roles came to be differentiated neither on the basis of seniority (senior and assistant ministers) nor of internal functions (pastor and minister of education) but of parish life and social engagement in the wider community. The ministers involved then related themselves and their sponsoring congregations to various sectors of community life—youth, recreation, housing, and education.

With probing insight, in a letter about his work, one suburban minister urges this kind of division of labor for another reason:

> People were threatened by the many changes—and in particular the growing opportunities for minority groups. I see now that, as Lifton says, "in order for learning to take place there must be enough security in the situation for a person to feel able to look at ideas or feelings which are threatening him." This is my thought: if there could be in a typical suburban setting . . . one pastor who carries out the traditional role—encourager, caller, counselor, guide to all the traditional events of the parish—and another who might work with two or three different suburban (and inner city) churches as a sort of stimulator, correlator, encourager of the pastors . . . then possibly something very creative could happen. . . . I wonder if this sort of two-pronged leadership is not an essential ingredient in every alive suburban parish today.[89]

Ecumenical Centers

Defending a church bureaucracy against complaints that it was not initiating radical social change, an executive once argued that an elephant is too big to fly but nonetheless serves other purposes quite well. Parish churches, for all their significance, aren't built to do all things; nor are denominational structures. We have need for other forms of the church. One vehicle is the ecumenical center, exemplified in Wellsprings, Philadelphia, and Packard Manse, Boston. Financed by contributions from churches, foundations, and committed individuals, an ecumenical center is religiously based but institutionally independent of control by denominational authorities. A look at this model may suggest tactical moves by individual suburban churches, even though the typical congregation has limitations (and advantages) that the ecumenical center does not. Moreover, we might conclude that "every city should have one," and the alert congregation may want to initiate steps that lead to such a local center.

The ecumenical center is free to initiate or expedite community concern in a way that is virtually impossible for most parish churches. The center more easily transcends inherited boundaries, for example. Wellsprings started as a white Protestant-Catholic dialogue group, but it grew very early to include Jewish-Christian encounter in its life, and then moved to relationships with militant blacks as well. The center was located physically halfway between concentrations of suburbanites and the central parts of the city.[90]

What does an ecumenical center do? One primary pattern at Wellsprings and Packard Manse is the exercise of initiative on issues of public concern. After discussion and preparation, the center's staff brings an issue to the wider community for consideration and possible action. The center becomes a resource for programming in local congregations, for example, after such a concern is publicized in public discussions, programs of study, or social action. In somewhat the same pattern, the better-known Ecumenical Institute, centered in Chicago but operating out of several regional locations as well, can bring to a church an intensive educational program on contemporary theology and Christian action.

An autonomous ecumenical center is free to take on almost any controversial issue, relieved as it is of many of the pastoral and maintenance concerns of a parish church. At Wellsprings new movements that need an address, a telephone, and an office may move in to get a start. The center thus facilitates an important characteristic of a healthy free society—grass-roots organizations concerned with public issues. Wellsprings policy holds that after four months a new group must be reviewed and Wellsprings itself will "endorse," "sponsor," or "cooperate" in its relationship or will sever it altogether. Packard Manse, with a staff of three, also has a pattern of raising an issue and spinning it off for other groups to take up more permanently.

A thorough study of individual congregations, "underground" churches, and other groups of committed people whose functional role in a community parallels that of the ecumenical centers above would turn up scores of fascinating stories and many different kinds of community impact. A recent review [91] gives some indication of the breadth of style to be found. The Church of St. Stephen and the Incarnation in Washington is a predominantly black church of the inner city. Besides regular parish functions the church serves ecumenical "peace and freedom" needs. Black-led movements of many sorts can find a home there. Innovation in liturgy and flexibility in churchly form characterize the church. Communion is open. Members come from throughout the Greater Washington area and include Jews as well as Christians.

The Community of Christ, numbering about fifty, is another experimental group in Washington. Sponsored by the American Lutheran Church, it has among its members some Roman Catholics, including a few priests. It holds no property. It is a deeply committed group that has moved into the inner city to serve the neighborhood around it. Emmaus House, in New York City, serves as a gathering place for discussions of a wide range of issues across the black-white and Christian-communist borderlines. All three of these "churches" illustrate the way that certain kinds of witness are enhanced by loosening up institutional relationships and patterns. From them the church at large will continue to learn; in one sense they represent research and development laboratories for the churches; in another, small commando bands advancing out front here and there along the battle lines of Christian mission.

Midwife, Broker, Ombudsman

Other metaphors and models also illuminate the church's role in worldly action. Think of the church as midwife. New life constantly works its way out of old societal forms. The midwife doesn't create the new life, but she serves to facilitate the painful process of birth and to keep an eye on danger signals. The church does not dictate the shape of the new society. Technology plays an enormous role. Government, newly self-conscious groups like students and blacks, the increasing power of emerging nations—all these play a part. But the person and the common good in the midst of rapid change need a prophetic midwifery as these potentially explosive forces tug and push during times of labor. The advocate-midwife must possess a hopeful trust in the future and must be eager to facilitate the birth of new structures for the sake of human welfare. She must also be firm and wise by virtue of her experience with the risks and anguish of such labor at other times and in other places.

Jürgen Moltmann demonstrates how often Biblical Israel —old and new—lives by the promises of God: her life is undergirded by her hope. With such a faith the midwife-church should be enabled to find a role that is played neither by utopian revolutionaries nor by comfortable institutions with narrower interests in their own welfare.

Think of the church as a broker. The church often serves to help relate the functions of existing institutions to unmet needs. The church does not often administer large programs of public welfare or basic adult education. It is not called on to raise money for the character-building agencies of the United Fund. In today's metropolitan context, however, it has a vocation of prompting public concern that these other services be well supported. It cannot itself build all the apartments to meet the nation's housing needs among the poor, but it can function to stimulate government and the housing industry to assume that kind of responsibility.

One of the new models of the campus ministry could be called brokerage. More than a counselor to students, the chaplain and the church can help an institution relate its resources more effectively to the needs of its city and region.[92] One college chaplain has used his position on the campus to start university-based seminars for business and professional men of the vicinity, seminars that take up public issues in which both these groups and the university community are involved. Another campus religious ministry team sponsored for students and the public a series of forums dealing with moral decisions that the society must make as it plans for the future.

The power structure of "white" churches even yet occasionally acts as broker for black groups working their way toward autonomous power. A church executive at the state level commented on one project for which he had been a go-between: "This ought to be done by black people or by an integrated committee headed by blacks, but the state power structure doesn't yet trust the new indigenous group that is managing the project. So this we can do—act as a front, a guarantor." The Boston Industrial Mission has helped expedite relationships between black leaders and some electronics firms that invested capital and expertise to develop a plant in the ghetto.

The broker metaphor applies to voluntarism especially well. As a network across the metropolis, churches know of and can bring together inner-city needs and suburban resources. In the Washington riots of 1968 after Martin Luther King's assassination, the suburban churches served as receiving points for gathering food. The network had already been established as a resource for the Poor People's March. Inner-city churches were ready as distribution outlets and were open day and night around the clock for three straight days. One inner-city church served three thousand meals on the Sunday after King's death. The byproducts from such cooperative work are often profoundly meaningful. "They're human, they're warm, they're even feminine," said one surprised black Baptist working alongside some white Catholic nuns.

Yet another image comes from Scandinavia and politics. An ombudsman is an official who is accessible to the public

for complaints against the government and redress of grievances. In many instances the church legitimately sees its
role in similar terms. The Office of Communications of the
United Church of Christ on behalf of the black population
in the Jacksonville, Mississippi, viewing area, and in cooperation with black churches, contested license renewal of
a local TV station because the station had failed to give
coverage to black activities. In a heavily black region, for
example, broadcasts using local participants—teen dance
programs and *Romper Room*—had gone on for years without ever showing a black face. The station eventually lost
its license, and this church intervention has put other sta-
tions on notice with significant effect.

Representatives of several denominational pension
funds, owners of Kodak stock, spoke up on behalf of
Rochester's FIGHT at the Kodak stockholders' annual
meeting during the controversy between FIGHT and the
Kodak firm. Some theological seminaries and church bodies
were among the first to withdraw deposits from banks that
made large loans to the South African government, becoming ombudsmen of a sort on behalf of the blacks in a racist
nation halfway around the world. In a complex society,
when one system touches others in so many ways, the
church has a role in assisting institutions and corporate
men of power to see their responsibilities in moral terms.
As midwife, broker, and ombudsman it carries out this
prophetic function.

4. WHERE THE ACTION IS

Can anything good come out of Nazareth? Will anything
good come out of the suburban congregation? Stereotypes

picture suburban life and churches as dull and conservative, unproductive, away from the center of American life, and they contrast them to the contemporary activist spirit that wants to be "where the action is." The question is raised therefore, "Why invest religious concern in the suburbs, out on the edge of things?" Here we sum up some answers to such a question.

Look first at three ways the criticism appears. Society and culture are on the move in the centers of power, the criticism goes, not in the suburbs. The action is in Washington, in the university, on Madison Avenue, but not in Centerbrook and Ridgeview, those quiet places where people sleep at night and daily consume products and ideologies generated at the power centers.

Psychologically, men don't live in the suburbs, runs the criticism on a second point. (This argument ignores women and children.) The man of the household "lives" at the plant or office, and homemakers who have tried to get Dad's attention on evenings when he was especially distracted by his work are aware of what the commentators mean. Physically Dad came home; inside, he didn't make it.

Still other critics assume that people aren't likely to attend church much anymore, or that if they do, it is for the wrong reasons. Worship and church life are presumed to have lost their meaning. God is dead.

The suburban church can acknowledge the partial truth in these criticisms without going on the defensive. The culture does have strong urban centers of power shaping and forming it, and the local residential church needs to be aware of them. Washington and the university and Madison Avenue are not beyond the horizon of the alert church concerned for the total Christian mission. Investment in the mission of the church in Buena Vista or Pinewood is an investment in one part of a total mission that also includes cooperative church action at the "centers of power."

Moreover, suburbanites do live in many worlds and the boundaries of these worlds are no longer coterminous with the boundaries of any residential town. The suburban base is only one of many in which church mission can be carried on, although it is as yet one of the more viable. Coming to grips with issues of faith and responsibility is no easier at the ski slopes or the shopping mall, much as we need experimentation with religious ministry in such contexts.

As for worship in the local congregation, it is not today nor has it ever been the only form that expresses Christian faith. It has been the most explicit form for most of Christian history, however, and it is fair to assume that it embodies and serves Christian faith in ways that will not suddenly disappear. Changes and crises there will be in patterns of worship, in the style of "God talk," and in the shape of personal belief, but it is erroneous simply to identify change with decay.

In what ways can it be argued that the "action" is in the suburban congregation? What important functions are being served in this particular context?

1. Although we live in many worlds, spread across the landscape, we live in suburbia too, and in great numbers. The largest category of Americans lives there. Men *are* among them in their important roles as fathers, citizens, community participants. These are roles that the suburban congregation can more easily touch than the worker role and they are roles rich with moral meaning. Hate and fear can erupt at zoning meetings in the suburbs, or when a white neighborhood faces its first racial integration. Responsibilities for good education are to be shouldered in local communities, and it is there that personal and com-

munal stewardship of money in the affluent society is decided conscientiously or carelessly. It is there that people vote and decide to be an enclave or an open community. Urgent moral choices abound in suburbia.

2. The action is in suburbia in both Christian and family nurture. The residential community is the intensive-care unit of society, in this case not for the end of life but for the beginning. Nothing is demonstrated more dramatically by the psychological revolution of the twentieth century than the immense significance of love and nurture during infancy and childhood. It is the loving and nurturing capabilities of adults in the intimacies of the home, not social concern in offices in Washington and Madison Avenue alone, that make for the well-being of the next generation. The bedroom community has profound significance as a place where babies are nursed lovingly, kindergartners are sent tenderly off to their schoolrooms, losing little leaguers are comforted, and shy teen-agers are helped to brave the first date and look forward to romance and marriage with healthy confidence.

In the church the generations gather—old people and small children—in one of the few places this happens in middle-class society. Here we of the uprooted, mobile, suburban culture learn we have roots in a family that predates Ellis Island and the Mayflower—the family of God. Here we are called to be a community that accepts all kinds of people without report cards or paychecks rendering personal judgment. Here we gather explicitly to answer that "value-starvation" Maslow talks about, for we are an intentional community pledged to glorify God and to serve the neighbor.

"Where the action is" in the last resort might be tested with a question such as the following: What most fundamentally determines the quality of a culture? The religious perspective contends that what men see as ultimate reality so affects their behavior that the culture succeeds or fails on the basis of it—the criterion of success being quite different from material or political gain. This view asserts that the human world is not the product of blind material forces. It is built of intentionality and faith. Ultimate reality—the object of faith—is that which men trust beyond and through the worldly objects and relationships they experience. It is that which men represent in religious language and myth. It is that to which they give their final loyalty, and final loyalties ultimately shape the culture.

Man's faith is expressed in worship, in moral decision, and in personal disposition and life-style. If this religious assumption is correct, moments when persons are challenged to express and to reflect explicitly upon their faith are moments of very significant "action" in the world. Such expression and reflection may take place in quiet moments far less dramatic than the bustling activity of a marketplace or an assembly line or political caucus, although of course it may take place in those busy moments too. Actually, the personal encounter with faith and the battle with despair, as played out both in prayer and in social relationships, constitutes one of the most gripping experiences that most men meet. Commitments and values are perceived and developed in reflection that can occur as often in the suburban "retreat" from the secular city as in the busier moments of the workaday world.

Arnold Toynbee observed in the history of civilizations a pattern he also saw in the saints, that of withdrawal and return. Similar dimensions exist in normal personal life— the interior side and the active one. "Action" of a significant sort takes place in the interior crucible of the spirit as well as in the public one. One of the most powerful symbols of this in recent years was displayed in the two sides of Dag Hammarskjöld—the one seen in *Markings* and the other in his public life at the UN. Another highly ambiguous indication of it may be seen in the search for interior experience through the drug cult and in the upsurge of interest in Oriental religion among Westerners distanced from serious involvement with their traditional religious faith. The suburban church, placed as it is in the residential and leisure-time sectors of metropolitan life, is called to probe the interior level of human life.

We may restate the matter using engineering terms. In the process of industrial production, the raw materials, the power that drives the machinery, and the physical layout of plant and equipment are the more obvious aspect of "action." Behind all this, however, is another level of decision and planning making itself felt in the design and switching that direct the material process. These cybernetic processes may operate very inconspicuously, but they are crucial. Similarly, the furnace of a house provides the heat, but the setting on the small low-voltage thermostat is the key to control and comfort.

In a society, biological processes and natural resources undergird physical life. Social institutions such as families and business corporations and governments shape and guide life on the personal and social levels, although they in turn are affected by the availability of natural resources and by technological progress. At still another level, however, these political, economic, and familial institutions are shaped by man's symbol system, his conscious and unconscious ways of understanding the meaning and goals of human life, his relationships to "ultimate reality." From this level, various kinds of "control" affect the organization of the social institutions of men. Man's decisions as to how he develops and directs material and social forces are subject to influence from another realm—his "spirit," his moral sensitivity, his God-relation as it is put by the religious man. The church is called to celebrate and provoke insight and motivation in men in just this dimension.

In such a view, the "religious" life of a society is crucial, for religion is an explicit locus of attention to and reflection upon the ultimate ground of human life and the moral claims men experience in that ground.[93] Many other aspects of culture participate in this function within the society, of course—education, philosophy, civic ceremonial, political rhetoric. For the religious person, however, these concerns are gathered together in his grateful, believing attempt at faithful obedience to God's will for man.

Iceberg-like, a society's life and destiny depend on forces well below the front-page events on the surface. How men perceive their world, and represent it to themselves, is also part of the "action." The church must play some role in these events so that its message is not misunderstood as an otherworldly or merely private and personal affair; to use a phrase from Paul Lehman, "God is a politician" and his will is for justice in the here-and-now world. But beyond and through social engagement the church is called to prompt reflection upon men's operative intentions and dispositions and moral norms.[94] Explicit concern for these factors is the church's vocation wherever its life touches men. The suburban church has the potential to affect profoundly the quality of the culture as it fulfills this fundamental role. Here too is "action."

All the above is not to be read as apologetic for the *status quo*. Ours will hereafter be an "experimental society," in

Elting Morison's phrase, one using feedback from its own actions and institutions to modify the controlling instructions. We no longer envision a single permanent pattern of society. The suburban church needs to be on its toes; but it needn't be, like Leacock's horseman, galloping off in all directions. Being on its toes means that it will hold in mind its own vocation and will so adjust its institutional patterns and mission strategies so as best to serve tomorrow as today.

This book has suggested numerous innovations in church action. Many others of lesser importance are to be seen in suburban church life. Some of the small changes, already experimentally evident, can be seen as a response to the changing life-style of suburbia. They may change long-familiar patterns, but they should surprise no one who has observed the varied patterns in the churches' life in times past. *Item.* The enlightened population in upper middle-class suburban communities has less use for one-way communication than in the past. The men's Bible class lecture is virtually nonexistent in these congregations, and discussion groups of various sorts have taken their place. *Item.* The sermon, delivered to a captive audience without back talk, now seems less satisfactory as a liturgical deed, and postworship sermon discussions are on the increase. Back talk may precede the benediction as explicit reflection becomes part of the liturgical action itself. A guide for written comments on the sermon was provided in one suburban church, the comments to be mailed in during the week. *Item.* The coffee hour itself, in urban and suburban congregations that have few other natural contacts during the week, has near liturgical importance in many churches.

The changing social habits of suburbanites may necessitate another change in the future. The Weekend Away not only suggests more of the ski slope and other leisure-time ministries. Congregations back home are adding on mid-week services again or simply changing the Sunday service to Wednesday or Thursday evening. One church in Minnesota [95] did just this for an entire summer without a drop (or a significant increase!) in the church attendance. The seven-day interval for regular involvement in the church may be subject to change as well. Longer sessions of more intense reflection may become the pattern—monthly day-long retreats and discussions for certain groups of adults, for example.

Patterns of Christian education will inevitably undergo more changes in coming years. The distances and automotive habits in suburbia have made for a pattern of simultaneous Sunday church school and worship on a widespread scale. Family services were also a response to the familism that is so prevalent a part of suburban life-style. Projecting changes from these experiences and experiments would be largely a matter of guesswork. One way of understanding the change they represent is to suggest that the trend is away from long-term institutionalized programming and toward more ad hoc occasions for study or celebration or social engagement. Teen-age and students groups, for example, are attracted to "happenings," one-shot meetings for special films, tours, or work projects during vacations, and the casual style of the drop-in coffeehouse—programs that present a dramatic contrast to the institutionalized patterns of the once-popular Sunday evening meeting at the church.

On the basis of the reflections in this book two broader trends would appear to represent responsible evolution for the suburban church; these two emphases serve to summarize the implications of much that has been discussed. First, the suburban church will see itself less as the independent and isolated fellowship that it has tended to be and it will increase its participation in a web of metropolitan relationships. Feedback from volunteers in the city and from vocational involvement in various sectors of the city's life will be broadcast within the congregation. Participation in civic life and in action movements designed to humanize further the life of metropolis will be recognized and encouraged. The congregation will become more of a community institution in its "secular ecumenicity." The church will exploit its connectional denominational ties and its crosstown ecumenical relations. The Consultation on Church Union has evoked some cries of "superchurch," "too big." But if main-line Protestantism merges and can give us diocesan units whose boundaries are coterminous with medium-sized metropolitan areas, the opportunities for meaningful service and action through the church in metropolis would be many times enhanced. A small denominational office doesn't relate well to the mayor's office, to regional planning, or to the metropolitan university; but a broadly based institution, inclusive of rich and poor and outer- and inner-city residents of the metropolis, does. Such a connectional-ism may develop gradually with a lessening of denominational ties to state headquarters and increased concern for metropolitan ministries of various sorts.

Secondly, what we might call a theology of institutions will become more developed than it has been. Ethical reflection within the congregation has been far too much a matter of personal morality alone. It is for that reason that the charge of "white racism" was so misunderstood by many well-meaning Christians; they failed to see the institutional shape that racism took. One researcher looked at the literature and programs of our churches and found them almost always relating to adults in terms of individual ethics or the role of adults in a single social environment—that of the family. Rarely was there any talk of their place as stewards of power and influence outside the home—as citizens, as workers in unions, school systems, hospitals, or corporations. Yet in all these ways a man is also called to invest himself for the neighbor's good in the human family and not only at home with his wife and children.

All this having been said, we must again revert to the central function of the church. The churchman who wonders anxiously what the church is all about because it doesn't seem to be changing things the way a corporation executive or an urban renewal agency can change things has not understood the vocation of the church. The church is called to help man and his society remember and respond to the ultimate reality of the God-relation. It does this in the twin aspects of its inner life (worship, teaching, and the concerned fellowship) and its public, parabolic social action. It hopes for the impossible possibility of making the world into the Kingdom, the arena of God's ruling. Every congregation of people attending upon Word and Sacrament has a right to feel that right there, as they wait for marching orders, they are where the action is. Such a view is expressed symbolically when it is said that in the Catholic Mass the crucial center point of all history is in some sense reenacted. That is where the action is, in suburb and city and country hamlet.

The church has a song to sing and a story to tell. In this book we have dealt largely with the active way of responsibly living out the story as a suburban institution. We must not, however, overlook the singing and the other ways we tell the story. A good novel has different levels of meaning; so too does Christian action. At one level there is the story, the yarn, worth reading for its own sake. At another there is the inner drama, among and within the lives of persons in the story. At a still deeper level, the conflicts and images and events of the story evoke symbolic meaning that are assertions about the nature of the cosmos itself. The social engagement of suburban churches through relationship to metropolis is worthwhile in its own right. A deeper vision of this action however, sees it as part of the song and the story, framing the meaning of Christian selfhood and community in the grace and graciousness of God.

"It was there from the beginning; we have heard it; we have seen it with our own eyes; we looked upon it, and felt it with our own hands; and it is of this we tell. Our theme is the word of life. This life was made visible; . . . What we have seen and heard we declare to you, so that you and we together may share in a common life, that life which we share with the Father and his Son Jesus Christ." (I John 1:1-4, NEB.)

Notes

1. Donald B. Meyer, *The Protestant Search for Political Realism, 1919–1941* (University of California Press, 1960), p. 61.

2. Quoted by Michael Harrington, *Towards a Democratic Left* (The Macmillan Company, 1968), p. 283.

3. Cf. Joachim Jeremias, *The Parables of Jesus* (Rev. ed., Charles Scribner's Sons, 1963), pp. 124–146.

4. Kenneth Keniston, *The Uncommitted: Alienated Youth in American Society* (Delta Books, Dell Publishing Company, 1960), p. 251.

5. Paul Goodman, *Growing Up Absurd* (Vintage Books, Random House, Inc., 1960), p. 202.

6. Herbert J. Gans, *The Levittowners* (Pantheon Books, Inc., 1967), p. 206.

7. *Ibid.,* p. 215.

8. C. Wright Mills, *White Collar* (Oxford University Press, Inc., 1956), p. ix.

9. A. H. Maslow, "A Theory of Metamotivation: The Biological Rooting of the Value-life," *Psychology Today,* July, 1968, p. 58.

10. Goodman, *op. cit.,* p. 12.

11. Gans, *op. cit.,* pp. 359 ff.

12. William A. Holmes, *Tomorrow's Church: A Cosmopolitan Community* (Abingdon Press, 1968), pp. 144 ff.

13. Keniston, *op. cit.,* p. 205.

14. A. C. Spectorsky, *The Exurbanites* (J. B. Lippincott Company, 1955), p. 228.

15. A study released by Bernard E. Ury Associates of Chicago—a public relations firm.

16. Keniston, *op. cit.*, p. 280.

17. See, for example, Erik Erikson, *Childhood and Society* (W. W. Norton & Company, Inc., 1950), Ch. 2, "The Theory of Infantile Sexuality."

18. A helpful book for church groups that wish to review family structure and the roles of men and women in home and community contexts is Gibson Winter, *Love and Conflict* (Doubleday & Company, Inc., 1956).

19. Keniston, *op. cit.*, p. 290.

20. Erikson, *op. cit.*, p. 250.

21. A. H. Maslow, *Motivation and Personality* (Harper & Brothers, 1954), p. 95.

22. Barrington Congregational.

23. For a part of the emphases in this and paragraphs that follow I am indebted to an article by Peggy Way, "Women in the Church," *Renewal*, October, 1964.

24. S. Williams, "Negotiating Investment in Emerging Countries," *Harvard Business Review*, January-February, 1965, pp. 90–91. For other materials that cite cases in business ethics, cf. Cameron Hall, *On-the-Job Ethics* (National Council of Churches of Christ in the U.S.A., 1963); Luther Hodges, *The Business Conscience* (Prentice-Hall, Inc., 1963); Raymond C. Baumhart, *An Honest Profit* (Holt, Rinehart and Winston, Inc., 1968); and Scott Paradise, *The Detroit Industrial Mission: A Personal Narrative* (Harper & Row, Publishers, Inc., 1968).

25. Keniston, *op. cit.*, p. 74.

26. John Galbraith, *The New Industrial State* (Houghton Mifflin Company, 1967), p. 343.

27. Spencer Klaw, *The New Brahmins* (William Morrow and Company, 1968), p. 263.

28. Lord Keynes, *Essays in Persuasion* (Preface), quoted by Stephen Toulmin, *Reason and Ethics* (London: Cambridge University Press, 1960), p. 181.

29. Edwin D. McLane, *The 7:05 and the Church Alive* (Prentice-Hall, Inc., 1963).

30. Rev. R. Bricker Gibson, now of Worcester, Massachusetts.

31. A superb account of his work in DIM is offered by Scott

Paradise, *Detroit Industrial Mission: A Personal Narrative* (Harper & Row, Publishers, Inc., 1968) . Cameron Hall, *On-the-Job Ethics* (Division of Church and Economic Life, National Council of the Churches of Christ in the U.S.A., 1963) , is a report on some discussion groups of the sort found in industrial missions, organized in this case in several other contexts.

32. *New Haven Register,* Nov. 9, 1968.

33. Grace Ann Goodman, *Rocking the Ark* (Division of Evangelism, Board of National Missions, The United Presbyterian Church in the U.S.A., 1968) , p. 167.

34. T. S. Eliot, "Choruses from the Rock," *The Complete Poems and Plays, 1909–1950* (Harcourt, Brace and World, Inc., 1952) , p. 103.

35. *The New York Times,* Nov. 13, 1968.

36. *Report of the National Advisory Commission on Civil Disorders* (called the Kerner Report) , p. 203.

37. *Ibid.,* pp. 1, 2.

38. Citation by Joseph Hough, *White Protestants and Black Power* (Oxford University Press, Inc., 1968) , from Benjamin J. Wattenberg and Richard M. Scammon, *This USA* (Doubleday, & Company, Inc., 1965) , p. 282.

39. "The White Exodus to Suburbia Steps Up," *The New York Times Magazine,* Jan. 7, 1968, p. 88.

40. "White population of central cities declined 1.3 million instead of rising 3.6 million as it would if it had grown at the same rate as the entire white population." (Kerner Report, p. 246.)

41. See, for a fictional but realistic account of this kind of resistance, Keith Wheeler, *Peaceable Lane* (Signet Books, The New American Library of World Literature, Inc., 1961) .

42. See Hough, *op. cit.,* for a discussion of Black Power, Negro pluralism, and the options for minority-majority relationships, especially pp. 15 ff.

43. See David McEntyre, *Residence and Race* (University of California Press, 1960) . As an example, one study of 34 neighborhoods, with matched neighborhoods as controls, showed 41 percent more or less the same in resale prices, 44 percent relatively higher than the controls, only 15 percent significantly lower (5 to 9 percent) . About ten thousand sales prices were

involved in the study; the San Francisco and Philadelphia areas were studied. See pp. 160 ff. Gans reports that the lower-middle-class homes of Levittown sold after nondiscriminatory policies were instituted without significant difficulty.

44. Alice Miel and Edwin Kiester, Jr., *The Short-changed Children of Suburbia* (Institute of Human Relations Press, 1967), p. 15.

45. *Ibid.*, pp. 23 ff.

46. U.S. Commission on Civil Rights, *Racial Isolation in the Public Schools* (1967), p. 196.

47. Jesse Jackson, *Church in Metropolis*, Spring, 1968, p. 9.

48. A phrase from William J. Wolf in "Black Consciousness and Higher Education," an occasional paper from the Church Society for College Work, Boston, 1968.

49. *Ibid.*

50. Hough, *op. cit.*

51. Preston Williams, in comments on Black Power at Harvard Divinity School, Oct., 1968.

52. James Baldwin, *The Fire Next Time* (The Dial Press, Inc., 1963), pp. 107–108.

53. Gibson Winter, *The Suburban Captivity of the Churches* (Doubleday & Company, Inc., 1961), pp. 21–23.

54. Gans, *op. cit.*, p. 147.

55. *Ibid.*, p. 155.

56. *Ibid.*, pp. 37, 38.

57. The Underwriting Manual of the FHA of 1938, for example: "If a neighborhood is to retain stability, it is necessary that properties shall continue to be occupied by the same social and racial classes." Race-restrictive covenants were recommended until 1947. After 1949, positive views on open housing appear in the Manual. Cf. McEntyre, *op. cit.*, pp. 301–303.

58. Reported by Harrington, *op. cit.*, p. 129.

59. *Ibid.*, p. 104.

60. George Sternlieb, *The Tenement Landlord* (Urban Studies Center, Rutgers University), p. xiii, quoted by Charles Harper in "Cooperative Metropolitan Ministries," a paper for United Church Consultation on Urbanization, St. Louis, Mo., April 3–5, 1967.

61. Cooperative Metropolitan Ministries, a Boston group, in

a study paper for the United Church Consultation on Urbanization, St. Louis, Mo., April 3–5, 1967.

62. Under programs of the 1968 Housing Act, a nonprofit housing corporation such as those which churches have organized can arrange housing beyond city boundaries, since this is a transaction between that corporation and the family, with federal assistance. Qualifying families pay as little as 1 percent interest on their mortgage loans if that amount itself brings their monthly payments up to 25 percent of their income; the Federal Government assumes the differential between the interest rate paid by the family and the market rate. Mortgages may be as high as $17,500 for families of 5 persons or more, $20,000 in high-cost areas. Families of relatively low income can now contemplate purchasing their own homes. The law provides for other kinds of assistance as well.

63. Proposals to this end are made by Charles Abrams in *The City Is the Frontier* (Harper & Row, Publishers, Inc., 1965).

64. Letter from Jane G. Wilhelm, Director of Community Relations, Reston, Va., April, 1969.

65. "Solving Problems in Urban Education," *Social Action*, Sept., 1968, pp. 10–11.

66. See, for example, *Project Concern: A Two-Year Report* (Hartford Public Schools, Hartford, Conn., 1968), p. 1; the role of the Council of Churches is cited.

67. Robert C. Wood, *Suburbia: Its People and Their Politics* (Houghton Mifflin Company, 1958), pp. 10, 13.

68. Reported by Harrington, *op. cit.*, p. 129.

69. Gibson Winter, *The New Creation as Metropolis* (The Macmillan Company, 1963), pp. 137, 139.

70. Benjamin Chinitz (ed.), *City and Suburb: The Economics of Metropolitan Growth* (Prentice-Hall, Inc., 1964), p. 134.

71. *Ibid.*, p. 115.

72. *Ibid.*

73. *Ibid.*, pp. 101–102.

74. See Herbert Gans, "The White Exodus to Suburbia Steps Up," *The New York Times Magazine*, Jan. 7, 1968, pp. 25 ff.

75. Constantine A. Doxiadis and Truman B. Douglas, *The New World of Urban Man* (United Church Press, 1965).

76. Jane Jacobs, *The Life and Death of Great American Cities* (Vintage Books, Random House, Inc., 1961).

77. James Gustafson, *Christ and the Moral Life* (Harper & Row, Publishers, Inc., 1968), p. 161.

78. See the lively booklet *By All Means, Mission: New Ministries from Old Churches,* by Grace Ann Goodman, (Board of National Missions, The United Presbyterian Church in the U.S.A.), pp. 6–16; *Rocking the Ark* by the same author reports several other congregations heavily engaged in mission through voluntarism.

79. See Abbé Michonneau, *Revolution in a City Parish* (The Newman Press, 1950).

80. Grace Ann Goodman, *Rocking the Ark,* p. 184.

81. *Ibid.*

82. Ministering groups within congregations and others drawn from across parish boundaries are described by Robert Raines, *New Life in the Church* (Harper & Brothers, 1961), pp. 126–127; and Alan Walker, *A Ringing Call to Mission* (Abingdon Press, 1966), pp. 75–96. See also Howard J. Clinebell, Jr., *Basic Types of Pastoral Counseling* (Abingdon Press, 1966), Ch. 16, "The Layman's Ministry of Pastoral Care and Counseling."

83. Cf. *The New York Times,* Feb. 10, 1969.

84. Saul Alinsky's work in establishing Chicago's Back of the Yards Council and the Woodlawn Organization have been well publicized. See his *Reveille for Radicals* (The University of Chicago Press, 1946) and Charles Silberman, *Crisis in Black and White* (Random House, Inc., 1964), Ch. 10. Useful descriptions of other community organization efforts are available. See John Fish, *et al., The Edge of the Ghetto* (University of Chicago Divinity School, 1966); Lyle Schaller, *Community Organization: Conflict and Reconciliation* (Abingdon Press, 1966). Robert Lee and Russell Galloway, *The Schizophrenic Church* (The Westminster Press, 1967), analyze the debates within a metropolitan church judicatory as it considers community organization.

85. Richard C. Cornuelle, *Reclaiming the American Dream* (Random House, Inc., 1965), quoted in a proposal for The Commons.

86. Grace Ann Goodman, *By All Means Mission*, pp. 27–37.

87. Winter, *The New Creation as Metropolis*, p. 103.

88. The story of Harold R. Fray's ministry in social action is a story all its own, reported in his *Conflict and Change in the Church* (United Church Press, 1969).

89. Letter from Rev. Winthrop Nelson, Jr., Nov. 3, 1968; a similar point is made by Robert Raines, *The Secular Congregation* (Harper & Row, Publishers, Inc., 1968), pp. 12–13.

90. Further description of Wellsprings is available in Raines, *ibid.*

91. Rosemary Ruether, "New Wine, Maybe New Wineskins for the Church," *The Christian Century*, April 2, 1969.

92. See Donald W. Shriver, Jr., "Towards Community in and Around the University," *Case Studies in the Campus Ministry* (Church Society for College Work, 1968).

93. One source in which this way of presenting the cultural and social system is concisely put is in Talcott Parsons, *Societies: Evolutionary and Comparative Perspectives* (Prentice-Hall, Inc., 1966), Ch. 2.

94. The terms are from Gustafson, *op. cit.;* see especially, Ch. 7.

95. Minnewashta congregation, Excelsior, Minn. Rev. Paul Flucke, pastor of this suburban congregation, reports deep satisfaction at the flexibility of the congregation in making this move, but not a strong conviction that life-styles yet necessitate repeating the experiment another summer.